The Shepherd Must Smell Like the Sheep

Written by

Dr. William L. Sheals

with Eric L. Ayala

This book is dedicated to the memory of my mother

Elma Sheals

One of the Good Shepherd's most beautiful sheep

End Touch Books a division of End Touch Movies, LLC
5805 State Bridge Rd #G115
Johns Creek, GA 30097

The Shepherd Must Smell Like The Sheep © 2013

ISBN-13: 978-1484158821
ISBN-10: 1484158822

First Trade Paperback Printing April 2013
Printed in the United States of America

This book is based on practical application from the New King James Bible. Several other sources were quoted and due credit given where appropriate.

For more information on End Touch Movies, LLC visit www.endtouchmovies.net

To contact Dr. William L. Sheals
Email: wia14@bellsouth.net

To contact Eric Ayala
Email: ayalawriter@gmail.com

Cover design: Ronny Myles » info@1badartist.com
Website: www.1badartist.com

Supplementary Editor: DJaye » journay2@gmail.com

TABLE OF CONTENTS

1. The Shepherd Must Be Available 7

2. The Shepherd Must Be Accessible 23

3. The Shepherd Must Be Approachable 34

4. The Shepherd Must Be Accountable 44

5. Ain't No Shame In My Tang 56

6. Lead By Example...61

7. The Lamb Slain..66

8. Motive and Spirit 75

9. GPS [God's Plan of Salvation] 84

10. Covenant Keeper..93

11. A Desperate Cry..99

12. The Blessings Of The Cross 103

13. Nothing But The Blood.......................................110

14. Business As Usual Is No Longer Acceptable 116

15. The Return To The Ultimate Shepherd................126

Jesus went through all the towns and villages, teaching in their synagogues, proclaiming the good news of the kingdom and healing every disease and sickness. When he saw the crowds, he had compassion on them, because they were harassed and helpless, like sheep without a Shepherd.

Matthew 9: 35-36 [NKJV]

"I do understand that as Pastors we are called to Shepherd God's sheep that comprise our individual flocks. I also understand that we are the Under-Shepherd to the Good Shepherd Jesus Christ. As ambassadors for Christ it is our duty to care for our flock liked the Good Shepherd commanded us in scripture."

Dr. William L. Sheals

1

THE SHEPHERD MUST BE AVAILABLE

So it was, when Jesus returned, that the multitude welcomed Him, for they were all waiting for Him.

Luke 8:40 [NKJV]

The people were waiting for Jesus because He made Himself available to them. They were anxious for His healing touch. They were excited for His ministry. He didn't ride in a special chariot. He didn't go a special route. He went directly to where He knew the crowd would be. Many times Jesus found Himself thrust into purpose even when He was tired and wanted to rest.

The life of Jesus teaches us very basic and fundamental truths about how we are to live and present ourselves as Christians. Jesus says in John 10:11; *I am the good Shepherd. The good Shepherd gives His life for the sheep,* and that's exactly what He did. For God so loved the world that He gave! It's interesting to note that the scripture refers to Jesus both as the Good Shepherd and the Lamb of God who became the ultimate sacrifice in the atonement for the sin of mankind. A sold out man or woman of God is to be offered up [unselfishly] to His service – that's what makes it a sacrifice; otherwise, we impede the call rather than further it. Purpose always draws us even when it's inconvenient.

I've often wondered, as a Pastor, how I would smell like a sheep if I couldn't identify with one. A Pastor by its very definition is the person who is to hold the lives and care of many people right in the palm of his or her hands. The dictionary claims that the word *Pastor* is an archaic word for *Shepherd*. I don't know that I would agree that the word is archaic, but I certainly would present a good argument that the Shepherd is and should be the one who cares, covers, mentors, nurtures, guides, and protects his flock.

Therefore take heed to yourselves and to all the flock, among which the Holy Spirit has made you overseers, to Shepherd the church of God which He purchased with His own blood.

Acts 20:28 [NKJV]

Many governments and military factions throughout the world swear allegiance to defend and protect their beliefs and the citizenship of their nation. In this country we also have an oath that is sworn by the military and our President to support and defend the Constitution of the United States against all enemies, foreign and domestic. They must affirm to bear true faith and allegiance to same. This declaration goes a long way in underscoring and mirroring the roles of the Pastor and Shepherd of God's nation. Satan is the enemy of that nation. As a Shepherd defends his flock against predators of the wild in the natural, we must take up our staff and defend our flock against our spiritual adversary – that is what we have sworn to do.

As the Good Shepherd, God sees to our most basic needs. As Under-Shepherd I must identify with the needs of the people I am charged with otherwise my service would indeed be useless. What good am I if I see someone hurting or lost and not lead them to a place of restoration, comfort, and safety? If I see a sheep who has stumbled and injured themselves I should be able to pick him up and help to carry the burden until he is able to stand and walk on his own again – this becomes particularly important to the younglings who have not yet found their footing. Those who are vulnerable to the attack of wolves or still susceptible to traps and are not yet grounded in the knowledge of the Word for themselves. If

I touch my sheep, if I comfort my sheep, if I identify with my sheep, then I will smell like my sheep and they will smell like me. I must be present and *available* to my flock in order to protect them.

> *Shepherd the flock of God which is among you, serving as overseers, not by compulsion but willingly, not for dishonest gain but eagerly;*

1 Peter 5:4 [NKJV]

Remember the story of the woman mentioned in the eighth chapter of the book of Luke who had a problem with her blood flow for twelve years. She was physically, spiritually, and financially broken. She'd spent all her money going back and forth to doctors who had no answers for her. But, when she heard that Jesus was coming she determined to get to Him no matter the consequences. She may not have had any money left, but she had enough faith to believe that all she needed to do was get to Him. She didn't wait to get to Him to apply that faith; the act of going exercised her faith. After pressing her way through the multitude of onlookers and hangers-on she got close enough to touch Him and when she reached out and grabbed hold of His garment the Bible records that immediately she was made whole. How did Jesus respond to her? He didn't look at her as if she'd lost her mind. He simply said; "Daughter, be of good cheer; your faith has made you well. Go in peace."

Can you imagine menstruating for so long a time? Can you imagine the pain she must've been in? Can you see the crowd pressing her on every side? Stepping on her. Ignoring her. How could this woman have gotten to Jesus if He wasn't available? How could she have gotten to Him if He wasn't accessible? How could she have gotten to Him if He wasn't approachable? Despite the throngs of people vying for His attention He recognized her touch, and her persistence paid off. She had heard that the Good Shepherd was nearby and she needed a miracle. She had faith enough to believe, and He had to be close enough for her to be able to get that miracle. Her faith and expectancy is what made her different. Jesus couldn't have been shielded by anything or anyone who felt He was too anointed to be around the very people He came to minister to. Imagine how this scenario would have played out if the disciples, or in this day and age, His armor bearers [body guards] would have pushed the woman away or kept her at arm's length – the outcome would have been quite different. She more than likely would have died with her illness, and so to would have those that were blind, lame, deaf, and literally lying at deaths door.

Jesus consistently presented a decisive model of the Shepherd/Sheep relationship throughout His ministry. The irony of His perfect example is that we have imperfect men and women attempting to live it out. As a walking, talking, breathing testament to how we are to exits Jesus hung out and ate with the rejected and disenfranchised. His assignment was to go after the lost [sheep], the unlovable ones and the disreputable ones that we still have little tolerance for. The pious Pharisees were beside themselves – accusing Him of being just like the outcast and wanting to do the things that they were doing – not unlike the good old finger-pointing "Christians" of today, right? But, Jesus knew something that so many of us have lost sight of; you can't get to the people who need ministering to the most if you're hidden behind the walls of elaborate sanctuaries "having church" instead of being the church. Jesus [the very incarnation of God] understood that if He was going to draw the lost He had to be among them – yet without sin. *Luke 5:32; I have not come to call the righteous, but sinners, to repentance.* What do you think we're here for? Are we better than Jesus? We are called to be the hands and feet of Jesus – that is our assignment.

Consider this; sometimes maintaining the house and making sure that the seats are filled costs us the truth and that skewered truth causes us to lose lives.

Unless the LORD builds the house, they labor in vain who build it;

Psalm 127:1 [NKJV]

THE SHEPHERD MUST BE AVAILABLE FOR ALL SHEEP!

It's amazing to me the number of churches that are being launched and the scores of Pastors and Bishops that are being commissioned yet en masse many sheep are still lost. Murder, sexual perversion, alcoholism, and drug abuse are rampant; not only in "the world" but right in "the church" and we the people of God, are still *having* church. One young minister shared with me that he's constantly being asked by people why he doesn't go out to Pastor his own church. So often leaders move because of outside voices and not the voice of God and wonder why their ministries are in shambles. Learn to search yourself far beyond your gifts or talents and make sure that you STAY IN THE FIRE until it's time for God to present you as pure gold.

A PASTOR MUST HAVE A TRUE SHEPHERD'S HEART AND BE PREPARED TO MINISTER BEYOND THE PULPIT; TOUCHING HIS SHEEP ON SUNDAY AND MONDAY!

In this you greatly rejoice, though now for a little while, if need be, you have been grieved by various trials, that the genuineness of your faith, being much more precious than gold that perishes, though it is tested by fire, may be found to praise, honor, and glory at the revelation of Jesus Christ.

1 Peter 1:6, 7 [NKJV]

Jesus charged us to go out. The action word here is *GO!* It is not a part of that directive to dress up on Sundays and sit in our grand cathedrals and praise the God we say that we love while society all around us is dying, lost, and scattered. That prostitute, or alcoholic, or drug addict, or the homeless and castaways are looking for the hope that we have in our hands to give – not just in words, but also in deeds. We must all, in one way or another be Shepherds in this regard. It's not only a Pastor's job or those that sit in a pulpit. We are all called to be available to minister this gospel of salvation and wholeness to those who feel they've been marginalized and are not welcomed to come into our carpeted, air-conditioned and marbled sanctuaries for fear of being further ostracized and looked down upon. If this is who we are, if this is what we do, then we are no better than the Pharisees who had a form of ritualistic worship but had no love in their hearts for the needy and the lost.

ONE COULD NOT TOUCH A PHARISEE BECAUSE OF HIS TITLE AND POSITION. TOO MANY OF US HAVE BECOME PHARISEES. NOT AVAILABLE AND UNABLE TO BE TOUCHED WHERE WE ARE.

'These people draw near to Me with their mouth, and honor Me with their lips, but their heart is far from Me. And in vain they worship Me, teaching as doctrines the commandments of men.' " When He had called the multitude to Himself, He said to them, "Hear and understand: Not what *goes into the mouth defiles a man; but what comes out of the mouth, this defiles a man."*

Matthew 15: 8-11 [NKJV]

Although many are set adrift by their own lust and desires, a great number of people attribute their lack of faith or interest in the church to the absence of love and compassion found there. In days gone by the church was the place of refuge, a 'safe haven'. Now it seems more likely to be the site of conflict and pain. Where it once stood as a hospital of sorts-where you would go to be healed- it can, more often than not, be the source of immeasurable hurt. It is no longer the mass articulation of love and compassion evidenced by its followers.

It is commonly held perception that some of us are phony, mean-spirited, unloving, bitter, and angry. And to many that perception is their reality. This perception is even applied to many Shepherds.

Confusing religion with relationship is another hindrance. *Religion* is a wall of derision separating us from Christ. *Relationship* is what draws us closer to Him. Our Christianity on its best day fails to come up to the standard that God has called us to. How can we say we love God whom we have not seen and shun our fellowman? Mr. *Bigstuff*, Mrs. *Bigstuff*, who do you think you are? Why do you think we're here? Extravagant churches, expensive suits, designer shoes, and the finest of educations are not going to save anyone. While I don't believe that God has issue with any of that, however when obtaining material possessions, titles and church status becomes more important than touching the unbeliever or those that are sick and tired of hearing our words and not seeing our actions, we have detoured from our purported mission.

The average man or woman [many sitting right in the church plagued with thoughts of suicide or dealing with issues of abandonment, loneliness, sexual identity, promiscuity or despair] is not concerned with how we can quote a scripture or break down text in Greek or Hebrew. They don't care how many degrees we have or how many letters follow our names. When a person is facing foreclosure or a medical crisis they just want to know if they can reach out to us when they need us the most.

Jesus said to Simon Peter, "Simon, son of Jonah, do you love Me more than these?"

He said to Him, "Yes, Lord; You know that I love You."

He said to him, "Feed My lambs."

He said to him again a second time, "Simon, son of Jonah, do you love Me?"

He said to Him, "Yes, Lord; You know that I love You."

He said to him, "Tend My sheep."

He said to him the third time, "Simon, son of Jonah, do you love Me?" Peter was grieved because He said to him the third time, "Do you love Me?"

And he said to Him, "Lord, You know all things; You know that I love You."

Jesus said to him, "Feed My sheep.

John 21: 15-17 [NKJV]

Feed them. Care for them. Love them. We as Christians are wasting our time by not following the example set forth by Jesus Christ. Are we really that important? Are we building houses [temples], and building ourselves up, and aspiring to things that ultimately won't matter? *All our righteousness is as a filthy rag.*

Why call yourself a Pastor if you're not available to the very people you Shepherd? One of the problems in the contemporary church is that most of us as Under-Shepherds have gotten away from what it means to be a Pastor. We don't make ourselves available in person anymore; mainly because of prosperity and financial gains or the size and scope of our churches. Some of us are spreading our ministries too thin. Jesus ministered for three plus years, and He knew that He could only be in one place at a time. He didn't try to Pastor in three or four places; that would have certainly encumbered His availability. As a Shepherd your congregation needs to be able to see you, touch you, be in your presence, and hear you on more than Sunday morning. Are you merely putting in an appearance like a rock star, whipping the people into a ten or fifteen minute spiritual frenzy, and then isolating yourselves behind a wall of bodyguards and gatekeepers as you are whisked away to appear before another assembly?

So he shepherded them according to the integrity of his heart, and guided them by the skillfulness of his hands.

Psalm 78:72 [NKJV]

Without operating in integrity and without humility in our calling we do a disservice to God, to ourselves, and to the people. We often lose sight of the fact that the same people who elevate you could be the very ones that tear you down. Remember the hordes that clamored for Jesus when everything was all good? Remember how many of them turned on Him when He was called before Pilate. The shouts of "Hosanna" suddenly turned into "Crucify Him!" Unlike so many of us He hadn't done anything wrong.

But He answered and said, "I was not sent except to the lost sheep of the house of Israel."

Matthew 15:24 [NKJV]

The Sheep

"May I speak to Pastor?"

"Do you have an appointment?"

"No, but it's really important."

"I'm sorry. Pastor is preaching out of town and won't be back until the end of the week."

"Nobody told me that when I called yesterday."

"He's got about five minutes before Bible study at the end of the month. Can I put you on his calendar?"

Indifference is among the primary reasons the sheep remain displaced. While it is unrealistic to believe that a Pastor, no matter how big or small the congregation is, can or should be at your beck and call any given hour of the day or night, there are times of desperation that you need to council with him personally – he is after all your Shepherd. If he is consistently tending another flock or is unavailable to you, you might want to reconsider your value to that ministry and your presence among those particular sheep; this may not be the pasture for you. Many find this to be the case. Constantly wandering from pasture to pasture [or church to church] grazing and feeding, hungry for hope, clinging to words, losing hope, losing heart, and ultimately giving up and going off alone to be devoured by despair. As a sheep, I wouldn't want to be in a pasture where I couldn't touch the Shepherd.

THE SHEPHERD MUST BE AVAILABLE. SOMETIMES EVEN JUST YOUR PRESENSE GIVES HOPE.

2

THE SHEPHERD MUST BE ACCESIBLE

What is a Pastor? How do we typically see ourselves? How do we perceive our role; and how do those perceptions inform our interactions with those we are appointed to Shepherd? Is it enough to have a certificate or degree from some esteemed theological institution framed and hanging on an office wall? Again there's nothing wrong with being a degreed and educated orator, but a Master's degree never destroyed a yoke and a Doctorate never saved anybody. We can't just talk the talk we must walk this thing out.

"Who may go out before them and go in before them, who may lead them out and bring them in, that the congregation of the LORD may not be like sheep which have no Shepherd."

Number 27:17 [NKJV]

In this modern age of technology a Pastor needs to try a bit harder to be accessible and personable. He needs to be present not just through the telephone, email, text, or tweets. In a very real sense the only way for the Shepherd to *smell* like his sheep is to roll up his/her sleeves and get his hands dirty. Being involved and a tuned in to what's going on within the flock is important. The most dynamic leaders don't just bark the orders they are at the forefront of the fight. This is not a competition or a popularity contest. We should not only cater to the congregants with the hefty check books but those, who like the widow with two mites, simply and wholeheartedly loves God. After all, it was her heart felt sacrifice that pleased God the most.

Here's what bothers me; some of my colleagues with large congregations boast that they don't baptize and don't do weddings unless it's for a staff member or relative. That's disturbing to me because it is a service that the Under-Shepherd has to offer. Surprising to many of my contemporaries I have my cell phone number and home number on business cards because I must allow myself to be available, accessible, and accountable to my congregation. If they need to talk to Pastor they have a right to talk to Pastor. I can't go on every call, hospital visit, birth, or wedding but in serious matters there is a mandate on this vocation to go. It is absolutely necessary.

I, therefore, the prisoner of the Lord, beseech you to walk worthy of the calling with which you were called, with all lowliness and gentleness, with longsuffering, bearing with one another in love, endeavoring to keep the unity of the Spirit in the bond of peace. There is one body and one Spirit, just as you were called in one hope of your calling; one Lord, one faith, one baptism; one God and Father of all, who is above all, and through all, and in you all.

Ephesians 4: 1-5 [NKJV]

There have been some great men and women of God who half kill themselves trying to be all things to all people; however, a good measure of grace comes with this calling to be able to carry out specific tasks. Honestly, since we cannot be omnipresent we can only govern what God has given us, do our very best with that, and let the Great Shepherd who is both omnipotent and omnipresent take care of the rest.

The concerned Shepherd never leaves the flock. If he does it is only to go after that one who has strayed and lost its way. In order to smell like the sheep the Shepherd keeps them close. He sleeps across the gate and guards them against any outsider that would seek to divide and destroy them – both foreign and domestic.

A sheep will not willingly follow a Shepherd from another flock. Herding and keeping the flock together is a full time job and requires an ever increasing amount of patience and prayer. Again, it is my conviction that no Shepherd can effectively Pastor more than one flock at a time. It's difficult to have several flocks to tender. Every flock has the same need for the gospel, and the truth, and for Jesus. But each flock is comprised of different dynamics and demographics. I believe you can minister or preach in more than one place, but you can't effectively Pastor – not and hold true to the designation of the office. If this is the case you're not "giving your life" to your flock. You haven't successfully met the people where they are. How can you feel the pulse of the people when you're not present? How can you raise disciples that will replicate themselves if you don't come before them in a Bible study? A thirty to forty minute message from the pulpit on a Sunday without understanding or exposition can't possibly be inclusive enough to reach the seasoned Christians, the baby Christians, and the unsaved that sit before you.

Jesus laid out the pattern of how we are to Shepherd when, after teaching the multitude, He took time to pull the disciples aside and pour into them personally. He was enlisting Under-Shepherds. In the upper room, before His arrest, before the last week of his life [John 14 – John 17] He spent quality time praying for and encouraging them to hold fast to the faith. They could see Him. They could hear Him. They could touch Him. He was not separated from them. His compassion was both tangible and palpable. As a Shepherd there must be time for that. Those who are called to serve as Under-Shepherds in the body of Christ must take that responsibility seriously. Otherwise, by the very definition, you're not a Shepherd/Pastor you're an evangelist.

The Sheep

What if Jesus had a *rider* [a contract replete with demands He needed to be met before He made an appearance] like some of our elitist gospel artists and preachers? I dare say that many of us could not afford Him. His honorarium alone could probably bankrupt the church. In truth financial disparity and seeing Pastors who prosper far above the congregation is disheartening for many. No church operates solely on prayer, but some ministries have influenced the Word to suit their own gain – marrying financial benevolence to salvation and favor. They make money their God and cause the people to lose faith in prayer, fasting, and living right leading the congregation to believe that you can buy yourself into God's choicest blessings. They love to use the slogan; "it's not equal giving but equal sacrifice", but how many times have you sat in a service where the preacher is calling for the hundred dollar line, and the fifty dollar line, and the twenty dollar line, and so on, linking such a sacrifice to the measure of your blessing and your faith.

Now, while some among us should be embarrassed wearing a hundred dollar dress, fashionable shoes, or suits and putting a couple of dollars in the offering such emphasis poured into the monetary does in fact shame those who just don't have it to give. Others simply use the statement as an excuse not to give at all. Money or the lack thereof remains the subject of great divide in the church and the misinterpretation of scripture which never said money was the root of evil, but the *love* of money is the root of evil.

The popular R&B group the O'Jays may have pressed this point a little further in their lyrics: *For the love of money people will rob their own brother. For the love of money people will lie, rob, they will cheat. For the love of money people don't care who they hurt or beat. Don't let money rule ya.*

Spending ten minutes in prayer and forty-five minutes to raise an offering is disgraceful. Have we lost our passion for God's presence? Celebrity and finance seem to be the rule and not the exception in today's church which has become the place for who's who gatherings to rival that of any Hollywood event. There is a ubiquitous attitude of arrogance that says *what's in it for me? What can I get out of this?*

Putting preachers up on unchallenged pedestals is what appears to set minefields in the church as we know it. There are many whose loyalties lie more with the personalities than the truth of the Word of God; following a man solely on the fact that he has charisma. The devil has charisma. A host of angels were kicked out of heaven seduced by his outward beauty and charisma. Preachers are just flesh and blood – as are we all. Subject to maladies and foibles and yes – even sin. Preachers are not God nor are they gods or deities of any sort.

But know this, that in the last days perilous times will come; For men will be lovers of themselves, lovers of money, boasters, proud, blasphemers, disobedient to parents, unthankful, unholy, unloving, unforgiving, slanderers, without self-control, brutal, despisers of good, traitors, headstrong, haughty, lovers of pleasure rather than lovers of God, having a form of godliness but denying its power.

2 Timothy 3:1-5 [NKJV]

"I must decrease so that God can increase" is another prevalent and repetitive pronouncement of the church, but in many instances God has been eclipsed by the man-made idols who eloquently and appealingly espouse the Word. Many church-goers [note the absence of the word Christian] run into problems when they bend over backward to glorify the Pastor – fervently seeking to be affirmed or validated by him or her. This can and has opened many misguided souls up to manipulation and abuse [mental, physical, financial, and sexual]. The God-void is then filled artificially by things never intended to fill it. Fleecing the sheep.

THE SHEPHERD MUST BE AVAILABLE IN THE SPIRIT OF RIGHTENOUNESS.

Therefore thus says the LORD God of Israel against the Shepherds who feed My people: "You have scattered My flock, driven them away, and not attended to them. Behold, I will attend to you for the evil of your doings," says the LORD.

Jeremiah 23:2 [NKJV]

In recent years many church leaders have come under attack and some have been openly condemned because of the sin that has been exposed in their lives. They've fallen from grace in the eyes of the people and many of the sheep, confused and turned off, have scattered or lost heart or faith in God. Had these disgraced ministers not been elevated into the absurdity of celebrity or held in such high esteem as to be perceived infallible or less than human, the error of their ways may not have been so catastrophic or damming to the body of

Christ. The devil set off a bomb of dissention in many congregations and just sat back laughing as the sheep ran to avoid the shrapnel. A divided flock became a conquered flock and the reverberation of destruction continued to echo as the sheep were marked for slaughter. Unfortunately the church as a whole is judged more so by the shortcomings of its people than the greatness of Jesus Christ.

For if we would judge ourselves, we would not be judged. But when we are judged, we are chastened by the Lord, that we may not be condemned with the world.

1 Corinthians 11:31, 32 [NKJV]

In the 34th chapter of the book of Ezekiel, he prophesies against the leaders of Israel, i.e, its kings, priests, and prophets. By greed, corruption, and selfishness, they had failed to lead God's people in the way He wanted. They were exploiting the people and using them for personal gain instead of helping them spiritually. Thus, they were responsible for Judah's captivity, and God would bring them into judgment. In contrast to the faithless Shepherds, Ezekiel went on to prophesy of a day when God would send a Shepherd after His own heart [i.e. the Messiah], who would truly care for the people. Rather than being manipulated or exploited the flock would receive "showers of blessings."

THE BLESSINGS – THE ANOINTING FLOWS FROM THE HEAD. IF THE HEAD IS NOT ACCESSIBLE, THE COVERING AND THE BLESSINGS ARE DELAYED.

"Whoever causes one of these little ones who believe in Me to sin, it would be better for him if a millstone were hung around his neck, and he were drowned in the depth of the sea. Woe to the world because of offenses! For offenses must come, but woe to that man by whom the offense comes!"

Matthew 18:6 [NKJV]

3

THE SHEPHERD MUST BE APPROACHABLE

He will feed His flock like a Shepherd; He will gather the lambs with His arm, and carry them in His bosom, and gently lead those who are with young.

Isaiah 40:11 [NKJV]

To borrow a phrase from the younger generation; *we got it twisted.* A Shepherd should be approachable and not segregated from the congregation by overzealous armor bearers, body guards, or his or her personality. I've noted that some parishioners don't feel comfortable speaking to their leaders. Some Preachers/Pastors demonstrate in their attitudes, mannerisms, and posture that they don't want to be touched as if, by the very act, they would somehow lose anointing. They are so far removed from their flock they're in a whole different zip code.

Question; if indeed you are anointed, who are you anointed for?

"All mankind is of one author, and is one volume; when one man dies, one chapter is not torn out of the book,

but translated into a better language; and every chapter must be so translated...As therefore the bell that rings to a sermon, calls not upon the preacher only, but upon the congregation to come: so this bell calls us all: but how much more me, who am brought so near the door by this sickness....No man is an island, entire of itself...any man's death diminishes me, because I am involved in mankind; and therefore never send to know for whom the bell tolls; it tolls for thee."

John Donne [1572-1631]

Now God worked unusual miracles by the hands of Paul, so that even handkerchiefs or aprons were brought from his body to the sick, and the diseases left them and the evil spirits went out of them.

Acts 19: 11, 12 [NKJV]

An air of superiority has also been noted as another reason or excuse why people tend to stay away from the organized institution called the church. This attitude is not only pervasive among leadership, but can and does permeate throughout the congregation. People were created to need one another. There are no big *I's* and little *You's*. You heard that one, right? Heard it, but it is seldom demonstrated. We may not all be called to the same tasks but we are all called to the service of Jesus Christ.

THE GREAT SHEPHERD WAS APPROACHABLE. THE UNDER-SHEPHERD MUST BE APPROACHABLE. THE SHEEP WILL FOLLOW THE SHEPHERD IN THIS ATTITUDE. WHEN YOU OBSERVE THE PULPIT THE REFLECTION OF SAME SHOULD BE IN AMOUNG THE CONGREGATION.

The Shepherd knows the sheep. The sheep know the Shepherd. A good Shepherd gives the sheep a sense of belonging. He affirms the sheep rather than being overly critical. He encourages the sheep rather than being discouraging to them. He instructs rather than condemning them. He speaks blessing over them rather than cursing them. He protects them rather than feeding them to the wolves. He gathers them together with the flock rather than scattering them in the wilderness. A good Shepherd brings healing. He is also willing to go after the lost sheep. A Shepherd grooms his sheep, keeps them clean and free of contamination from the world, the flesh and the devil. And yes, there are times when our stubbornness must be corrected.

CORRECTED WITH AGAPE LOVE AND IN THE SPIRIT OF CHRIST.

"My sons, do not despise the chastening of the LORD, nor be discouraged when you are rebuked by Him; For whom the LORD loves He chastens..."

Hebrews 12:5-6 [NKJV]

Wouldn't you rather be corrected by a loving and caring Shepherd as opposed to a vindictive and distant one?

The Shepherd's position is above the sheep in leadership only. Metaphors can be taken out of context as it relates to biblical truths. We must always guard against pseudepigrapha [counterfeit/sham] within our didactic teaching and instruction.

It is unfathomable that many times a person does not have to go outside the church to be beaten down, castigated, maligned or condemned to hell. The pulpit can sometimes become a soapbox or whipping board for our own ideas and agendas rather than a launching pad for the undefiled gospel of Jesus Christ. We should not use our positions to enslave the congregation with words that speak curses rather than blessings. Verbal abuse is never O.K. Manipulating scripture to fit our program is wrong.

For the time has come for judgment to begin at the house of God; and if it begins with us first, what will be the end of those who do not obey the gospel of God?

1 Peter 4: 17 [NKJV]

The Sheep

But when He saw the multitudes, He was moved with compassion for them, because they were weary and scattered, like sheep having no Shepherd.

Matthew 9:36 [NKJV]

The Shepherd must be vigilant and available to tend his own sheep. The model of the relationship between the Shepherd and the sheep has to be both natural and spiritual. Understandably as a congregation grows it becomes harder for the Shepherd to interact with each and every sheep on an individual basis but there should be some effort put forth. There should be balance. There are those within the congregation that are the proverbial wolf in sheep's clothing and a Pastor must be discerning and take great care when dealing with such, but discernment comes with being filled with the Spirit – not superiority. The ideal Shepherd needs to be relatable – plugged in to his/her flock. In this regard adequate face time is essential. Being approachable is mandated.

As an example of shepherding the flock for the past thirty-three years of pastoring I have purposely walked among my congregation before services to greet them; many I know by name and some I do not. But, this accomplishes two things; it allows me to see them and touch them and allows them to be able to touch me. My church is of some size and this may be one of the only times parishioners get to come in contact with me in a personal way. I don't do it for show. I do it because I have a genuine affection for them. I typically stand before them at offering time to allow additional interaction. Even after the preached Word when I've found myself overcome with exhaustion and drenched in perspiration I allow the sheep to see me and touch me. I try to speak further words of encouragement into their lives as they exit the foyer. I'm not saying that this is the prescribed way for all, but this is the call of God on *my* ministry. As Shepherds we must all find ways to be accessible, available, and approachable to our people, no matter the size and scope of the church.

THE SHEPHERD'S JOB DOESN'T BEGIN OR END IN A PULPIT WITH A MICROPHONE ON SUNDAY MORNING.

Although the Shepherd is in a position of authority the sheep still needs to see that he/she is genuinely concerned about the flocks wellbeing – not just on Sunday and not only when it's time to raise money for anniversaries or building projects. There needs to be some kind of interaction between Shepherd and sheep on a more personal level. Of course there are events and functions that cannot be attended by the Pastor of the church, but the flock needs to be assured that they matter and are not just among the faceless, nameless, hordes that assemble for a weekly or bi-weekly feeding.

A good Shepherd understands when the sheep are hurting or in trouble. He comes to their aid or to their defense when he's needed. When the sheep have messed up the Shepherd helps them to understand where they went astray. He helps them get back on track and shows them through scripture or example, if need be, how not to keep making the same mistakes over and over again.

When we think of the word *Shepherd* much of the time our go-to scripture is Psalm 23; *The LORD is my Shepherd; I shall not want. He maketh me to lie down in green pastures: he leadeth me beside the still waters. He restoreth my soul: he leadeth me in the paths of righteousness for his name's sake. Yea, though I walk through the valley of the shadow of death, I will fear no evil: for thou art with me; thy rod and thy staff they comfort me. Thou preparest a table before me in the presence of mine enemies: thou anointest my head with oil; my cup runneth over. Surely goodness and mercy shall follow me all the days of my life: and I will dwell in the house of the LORD forever.* While that is absolutely true and capsulizes our walk in Christianity it's by no means all that we are to expect. The scripture also tells us in Jeremiah 3:15 that *God will give us Shepherds according to His heart, who will feed us with knowledge and understanding.* Do you wonder how many of our Pastors today still seek the heart of

41

God? If so, should that make them more approachable or less so? There are several instances in the Bible when someone wanted to approach Jesus for council or healing and yes to call Him out for ridicule, but He was always approachable. Even in His last hour when the Roman soldiers came to seize Him they were able to get to Him without hindrance. That is of course unless you count Peter who was prepared to take up arms and took the ear of one of the soldiers. Certainly a good Under-Shepherd should hope to inspire this sort of loyalty from his congregants – if he/she indeed was equally devoted to those in his/her charge.

IF THE SHEPHERD MAKES HIMSELF APPROACHABLE TO HIS SHEEP, THE FATHER AND THE SHEEP WILL TAKE CARE OF HIM.

The congregation has a responsibility in this relationship as well. With the explosion of social media it's more convenient, and less complicated just to stay home and turn on the computer or tablet and surf to your ministry of choice online. If you don't like what one is saying, find another. But you are no more plugged into that congregation or Pastor than they are to you. Without a viable connection to the man or woman of God how can we expect to have them reach out to you if they don't even know who you are? You're not only invisible to them you're non-existent to the flock. Some even have the nerve to be offended when they've called for help and can't get it. You haven't been to the church since the day you decided to join, or your time in attendance is marked by special occasions such as Christmas, Mother's Day, and Easter. You can't expect the same level of ministry from a virtual Shepherd; you can't touch him and he can't touch you. Woe unto you distant sheep off in the pasture alone – doing your own thing. Connection to a building is not a connection to God. Membership has its privileges – but that is more than in name only.

Not forsaking the assembling of ourselves together, as is the manner of some, but exhorting one another, and so much the more as you see the Day approaching.

Hebrews 10:25 [NKJV]

4

THE SHEPHERD MUST BE ACCOUNTABLE

"Woe to the Shepherds who destroy and scatter the sheep of My pasture!" says the LORD.

Jeremiah 23:1 [NKJV]

The primary task of a Shepherd to his congregation is to feed [teach] them knowledge and understanding. The local church Shepherd is given by God, and he must take the full oversight in relation to his ministry He is to give the sheep directions from God's Word. A good Shepherd is invested in his flock's well-being and seeks to promote unity in place of loneliness and isolation. We should be about developing true connections. What good does it do any of us to be a mile wide and an inch deep in regard to our relationships?

Why am I impressed to drive this point? Simply put the Shepherd or Pastor is the leader and the one to cast the vision for the flock. Proverbs 29:18 says that without *vision* the people perish. The lack of a caring available Shepherd will cause many to separate, run amok, and cast off restraint.

As Shepherds first and foremost we must be accountable to God who has called us to this task and given us the flock to tend. I feel this is where most of us have lost our way. We've become legends in our own minds and not accountable to the people we serve. Does this mean that we are to open up every aspect of our lives to bear for observation and scrutiny, no of course not, but when you're not accountable to God then the people don't mean that much to you anymore. Accountability comes through humility. Humility draws us to service. How can you be accountable to the flock if you're not accountable to God or accountable to the Word?

The pursuit of titles, position, notoriety, and money eat away at the heart of accountability. Remember *the love of money is the root of evil.* When the love of money, the love of self-promotion and gain outweigh our love for souls – the love of serving – then it has taken root in evil and will bring about the misuse of everything and everyone at our disposal.

Simply by human error alone we can do so much damage unintentionally to the body of Christ. Not trusting God for the calling of the ministry has brought about the proliferation of store front churches hording sheep and seeking after mega church status. Some are looking at the fruit without considering what it takes to nurture the fruit to harvest. They recklessly plant the tree without considering how to raise it to maturity. Our job is to cultivate the ground, plant the seed, nourish the seed, and fertilize that seed. It may take years for fruit to bear, but if we attempt to raise a tree without taking the time to nurture it the fruit will not be good.

"Either make the tree good and its fruit good, or else make the tree bad and its fruit bad; for a tree is known by its fruit. Brood of vipers! How can you, being evil, speak good things? For out of the abundance of the heart the mouth speaks. A good man out of the good treasure of his heart brings forth good things, and an evil man out of the evil treasure brings forth evil things. But I say to you that for every idle word men may speak, they will give account of it in the day of judgment. For by your words you will be justified, and by your words you will be condemned."

Matthew 12:33-37 [NKJV]

We are responsible for souls. When our focus is not on our flock – when our focus is not on providing teaching and nourishment for the people that leaves the gate wide open for the devil and he does his job all too well.

In Shakespeare's Henry IV, Part 2, Act 3, Scene 1, the king has a soliloquy. It begins, "How many thousands of my poorest subjects are at this hour asleep! O sleep, O gentle sleep…". At the end, he declares, "Uneasy lies the head that wears a crown."

The burden of the people is weighty. Their care is sometimes costly. Many times to the Shepherds own lacking, but this is a mantle designed by God to those who are called to the work. If the call is not pure then the accountability will be non-existent and therefore bring about the potential to bastardize the office.

The Emperor's New Clothes [*This article is about the story by Hans Christian Andersen*]

A vain Emperor who cares for nothing but his appearance and attire hires two tailors who are really swindlers that promise him the finest, best suit of clothes from a fabric invisible to anyone who is unfit for his position or "just hopelessly stupid". The Emperor cannot see the cloth himself, but pretends that he can for fear of appearing unfit for his position; his ministers do the same. When the swindlers report that the suit is finished, they mime dressing him and the Emperor then marches in procession before his subjects, who play along with the pretense. Suddenly, a child in the crowd, too young to understand the desirability of keeping up the pretense, blurts out that the Emperor is wearing nothing at all and the cry is taken up by others. The Emperor cringes, suspecting the assertion is true, but holds himself up proudly and continues the procession.

Wikipedia

PRETENDING TO BE ACCOUNTABLE AND CARING BY TRYING TO LIVE UP TO A TITLE OR POSITION IS FOOLISH PRIDE. TODAY MANY SHEEP SEE BEYOND THE SUIT AND THE PRETENSE. THEY SEE THE ABSENCE OF ACCOUNTABILITY MERELY BY THE ABSENCE OF THE SHEPHERD.

Pride goes before destruction and a haughty spirit before a fall. Better to be of a humble spirit with the lowly, than to divide the spoil with the proud.

Proverbs 16: 18, 19

I know we as Christians are all responsible and accountable for those that we drive away or bring to Christ, but being a Shepherd/Preacher/Pastor carries its own hefty responsibility. Pretense and piously living a life that is unaccountable to anyone is dangerous. I wouldn't want to claim a calling to the ministry that wasn't appointed by God Himself. It is absolutely nothing to take lightly. To whom much is given much is required – and God meant that thing!

Irresponsible Shepherds

And the word of the LORD came to me, saying, "Son of man, prophesy against the Shepherds of Israel, prophesy and say to them, 'Thus says the Lord GOD to the Shepherds: "Woe to the Shepherds of Israel who feed themselves! Should not the Shepherds feed the flocks? You eat the fat and clothe yourselves with the wool; you slaughter the fatlings, but you do not feed the flock. The weak you have not strengthened, nor have you healed those who were sick, nor bound up the broken, nor brought back what was driven away, nor sought what was lost; but with force and cruelty you have ruled them. So they were scattered because there was no Shepherd; and they became food for all the beasts of the field when they were scattered. My sheep wandered through all the mountains, and on every high hill; yes, My flock was scattered over the whole face of the earth, and no one was seeking or searching for them."

Therefore, you Shepherds, hear the word of the LORD: "As I live," says the Lord GOD, "surely because My flock became a prey, and My flock became food for every beast of the field, because there was no Shepherd, nor did My Shepherds search for My flock, but the Shepherds fed themselves and did not feed My flock"— therefore, O Shepherds, hear the word of the LORD! Thus says the Lord GOD: "Behold, I am against the Shepherds, and I will require My flock at their hand; I will cause them to cease feeding the sheep, and the Shepherds shall feed themselves no more; for I will deliver My flock from their mouths, that they may no longer be food for them. "

Ezekiel 34: 1-10 [NKJV]

The Sheep

"What do you think? If a man has a hundred sheep, and one of them goes astray, does he not leave the ninety-nine and go to the mountains to seek the one that is straying?

Matthew 18:12 [NKJV]

Transparency affects the Shepherd/sheep relationship in a big way. From the exalted perch of a pulpit pontificating about the woes of the world and where one should be in their walk with Christ it isn't easy to ascertain whether or not the Shepherd understands or even cares what the sheep are dealing with.

Sheep have been known to be dumb, unimaginative animals for blindly following the leader without question, but it begs the question; should it be so? There are also multiple personalities within the fold that certainly can't make the job any easier for a Shepherd to deal with. The Shepherd should know the peculiarities of his flock; ergo multiple flocks shepherded caringly by one man is next to impossible. There's too much at stake. There are little ones and [spiritual] cripples that he/she must carry until they are able to stand and walk on their own. There are nursing ones that won't be hurried. Old sheep that can barely get along, and those who always want to be out front – the bullies that butt and push to get their way. The timid ones; those that are afraid to follow. There are some sheep in any fold that no matter how they are coaxed and directed will always find something disagreeable. They can always find some way to buck against the flow and direction of the rest of the flock and in so doing cause disruption and discourse. This is no less true of the church. In such cases the Shepherd must have keen insight and discernment to understand what he is dealing with. Jesus exhibited a great many qualities that we are to take to heart as Christians as we do the work He's set before us and win back the lost. Above all things that Jesus was, He was compassionate. Many who have left the church and rejected the faith have done so because of the lack of compassion.

Several who count themselves among those who proclaim to love God but have no use for the fame games or spiritual acrobatics [jumping through hoops] of the church attribute their apathy to what they've deemed as "pimps in the pulpit".

Pastors have been known to say that they know how to work a crowd in order to get them to do what they want that is not what the Bible mandates. Once assembled we all play a part in the biggest game of Simon Says known to man. Touch your neighbor and say this, that, or the other thing has become as common as punctuation at the end of a sentence. Are we speaking words of life or are we speaking damnation? Are we listening to what we're being asked to do? Are we doing it just because *Simon* said?

In Second Timothy we are instructed to study to show ourselves approved unto God, a workman that need not to be ashamed, rightly dividing [appropriately understanding] the word of truth. Does this mean that we shouldn't heed what the Pastor or Shepherd designated to feed our souls is delivering; I think not. But it does indicate that we are to know Him for ourselves; after all the burden of our salvation is ours alone. *Work out your own soul salvation with fear and trembling.* It is imperative that we develop, nurture, and cultivate our own relationship [not religion] with the Chief Shepherd Jesus Christ. In this regard the Shepherd cannot be held solely responsible.

Again the sheep have a good deal of the responsibility in the relationship with the Shepherd. The Shepherd can lead us to the water and feed us, but only sheep can make other sheep. Anybody can be a member of a church, but there comes a time when membership should translate into discipleship. We must take the words of knowledge and salvation that are imparted to us and share the message of salvation with others. That is our great commission.

Fear God and keep His commandments, for this is man's all. For God will bring every work into judgment, including every secret thing, whether good or evil.

Ecclesiastes 12:13 [NKJV]

And that's just not for the Pastor; that is for all of us!

Although many stray from the truth and false teachings surreptitiously slip into the church, God's purpose for His faithful followers cannot be thwarted. When Jesus said to

Peter *upon this rock I will build my church*, the rock – the foundation was Jesus Himself. The church is not brick and mortar – it's us – the people. The foundation of God, i.e. the church, cannot be destroyed because it is built on the Word and it is on that Word that we are to stand.

Finally, my brethren, be strong in the Lord and in the power of His might. Put on the whole armor of God, that you may be able to stand against the wiles of the devil. For we do not wrestle against flesh and blood, but against principalities, against powers, against the rulers of the darkness of this age, against spiritual hosts of wickedness in the heavenly places. Therefore take up the whole armor of God, that you may be able to withstand in the evil day, and having done all, to stand.

Ephesians 6: 10-13 [NKJV]

5

Ain't No Shame In My Tang

Many of us are old enough to remember *Tang* as that fruit-flavored powdered drink that was first marketed in 1959 and was used as the official beverage for astronauts in the NASA space program in 1962. It may also be of interest to note that one of the definitions of *tang* according to the dictionary is *a long and slender projecting strip, tongue or prong forming part of an object, as a chisel, file, or knife, and serving as a means of attachment for another part, as a handle or stock.*

But now indeed there are many members, yet one body. And the eye cannot say to the hand, "I have no need of you"; nor again the head to the feet, "I have no need of you." No, much rather, those members of the body which seem to be weaker are necessary. And those members of the body which we think to be less honorable, on these we bestow greater honor; and our unpresentable parts have greater modesty, but our presentable parts have no need. But God composed the body, having given greater honor to that part which lacks it, that there should be no schism in the body, but that the members should have the same care for one another. And if one member suffers, all the members suffer with it; or if one member is honored, all the members rejoice with it.

1 Corinthians 12:20-26 [NKJV]

So, where am I going with this? In this instance *tang* refers to the tongue, protruding from ones mouth, attached to ones face, and connected to the body. The tongue cannot operate apart from the mouth and the mouth, although it wants to much of the time, cannot operate apart from the body. Rogue sheep are of no use to the body of Christ and can be extremely detrimental. They use that protruding strip with complete abandon, tearing down what God is trying to build. Conversely a Shepherd with no flock of his own to tend can do an equal amount of damage – scavenging and reaping sheep from another's herd attempting to build what God never intended.

Death and life are in the power of the tongue, and those who love it will eat its fruit.

Proverbs 18:21 [NKJV]

You did know that Pastors are a part of the five-fold ministry ordained by God, didn't you? It's not a man-made position. Not if you are truly to be led by the Spirit of God.

And He Himself gave some to be apostles, some prophets, some evangelists, and some Pastors and teachers, for the equipping of the saints for the work of ministry, for the edifying of the body of Christ, till we all come to the unity of the faith and of the knowledge of the Son of God, to a perfect man, to the measure of the stature of the fullness of Christ;

Ephesians 4:11 [NKJV]

So why abuse the post of the Shepherd/Pastor? Why use your *tang* to mislead for the sake of notoriety and position? The Shepherd is not the one to be glorified. The man is not greater than the calling because it is God who called the man.

As discussed in previous chapters as Shepherds we are to take particular care with those in our charge; not just in what we do but in what we say.

"Most assuredly, I say to you, he who does not enter the sheepfold by the door, but climbs up some other way, the

same is a thief and a robber. But he who enters by the door is the Shepherd of the sheep. To him the doorkeeper opens, and the sheep hear his voice; and he calls his own sheep by name and leads them out. And when he brings out his own sheep, he goes before them; and the sheep follow him, for they know his voice. Yet they will by no means follow a stranger, but will flee from him, for they do not know the voice of strangers." Jesus used this illustration, but they did not understand the things which He spoke to them.

Then Jesus said to them again, "Most assuredly, I say to you, I am the door of the sheep. All who ever came before Me are thieves and robbers, but the sheep did not hear them. I am the door. If anyone enters by Me, he will be saved, and will go in and out and find pasture. The thief does not come except to steal, and to kill, and to destroy. I have come that they may have life, and that they may have it more abundantly.

John 10:1-10 [NKJV]

Have we gotten too comfortable with God? Have we gotten too comfortable with sin? Our words are not just words. Our lives need to reflect what we're saying. People are tired of the rhetoric. If the model of the church [and I'm not taking about the physical building] is no better than what is being seen in the world, we [the church] don't matter. If leaders continue to say one thing and live another then our preaching is vanity. If we the people don't align ourselves with God, and say what He says, we may as well close the doors of the physical structure. Let's set aside hypocrisy and judgments. If we're not going to be the embodiment of change, talking about it just won't cut it.

With loving kindness have I drawn you; says the Lord. What life have you led or words have you spoken that would bring an unbeliever closer to God? What have you done that would drive them further away?

For whosoever shall call upon the name of the Lord shall be saved. How then shall they call on him in whom they have not believed? And how shall they believe in him of whom they have not heard? And how shall they hear without a preacher? And how shall they preach, except they be sent?

Romans 10: 13-15 [NKJV]

6

LEAD BY EXAMPLE

*Then the apostles gathered to Jesus and told Him all
things, both what they had done and what they had taught.
And He said to them, "Come aside by yourselves to a
deserted place and rest a while." For there were many
coming and going, and they did not even have time to eat. So
they departed to a deserted place in the boat by themselves.*

*But the multitudes saw them departing, and many knew
Him and ran there on foot from all the cities. They arrived
before them and came together to Him. And Jesus, when He
came out, saw a great multitude and was moved with
compassion for them, because they were like sheep not having
a Shepherd. So He began to teach them many things. When
the day was now far spent, His disciples came to Him and
said, "This is a deserted place, and already the hour is late.
Send them away, that they may go into the surrounding
country and villages and buy themselves bread; for they have
nothing to eat."*

But He answered and said to them, "You give them something to eat."

And they said to Him, "Shall we go and buy two hundred denarii worth of bread and give them something to eat?"

But He said to them, "How many loaves do you have? Go and see."

And when they found out they said, "Five, and two fish."

Then He commanded them to make them all sit down in groups on the green grass. So they sat down in ranks, in hundreds and in fifties. And when He had taken the five loaves and the Two fish, He looked up to heaven, blessed and broke the loaves, and gave them to His disciples to set before them; and the two fish He divided among them all. So they all ate and were filled.

Mark 6: 3-42 {NKJV]

Again the Good Shepherd gives us another powerful example of smelling like the sheep. Even after successful ministry missions Jesus was moved with compassion [there's that word again] by the spiritual hunger and the physical hunger of His sheep.

- The Good Shepherd made Himself **available** [vs. 33]. He was with them.
- The Good Shepherd made Himself **accessible** [vs. 34]. He was leading them.
- The Good Shepherd made Himself **approachable** [vs. 35,36]. They were all around him.
- The Good Shepherd made Himself **accountable** [vs. 37-42]. He brings them to still waters, food, and safety.

A true Shepherd loves his flock enough to be transparent. He does not rule from the mountaintop apart from them, but rather close enough to lead and protect. If we are to truly be leaders, not only in the eyes of the church but in the eyes of the world, we must be the standard of all that is called Godly.

For the earnest expectation of the creation eagerly waits for the revealing of the sons of God.

Romans 8:19

If we are not the standard bearers pointing the lost sheep to Jesus Christ, then who will? If not now, when? It can't be emphasized enough that we need to stop quoting the Word and start living the Word. We were called to be the voice, the hands, and the feet of Jesus. The message has been tainted by smoke and mirrors – stunts and gimmicks. The world doesn't care anymore what the church has to say because they see what the church is doing. We are supposed to be the light of the world, not in the spotlight of scandal and deception. We are supposed to be the salt of the earth, not salt substitute. *The church will continue to be irrelevant and mocked as long as we remain divided.*

The only way the body of Christ is going to see growth and change is when we start meeting people where they are. Loving them where they are. Commit to walk with them in love and disciple them through their journey.

For all have sinned and fall short of the glory of God, but it is the strength of our character and our commitment to salvation that causes us to get up no matter how many times we fall.

7

The Lamb Slain

All who dwell on the earth will worship him, whose names have not been written in the Book of Life of the Lamb slain from the foundation of the world. If anyone has an ear, let him hear.

Revelation 13: 8-9 [NKJV]

Yom Kippur also known as **Day of Atonement** is the holiest day of the year for the Jewish people. Its central themes are atonement and repentance. Jewish people traditionally observe this holy day with a 25-hour period of fasting and intensive prayer, often spending most of the day in synagogue services. Yom Kippur completes the annual period known in Judaism as the High Holy Days or Yamim Nora'im ["Days of Awe"].

Yom means "day" in Hebrew and *Kippur* comes from a root that means "to atone". Atonement was simply the act of bringing the people who had sinned back into alignment with God.

Yom Kippur is the tenth day of the month of <u>Tishrei</u> and also regarded as the "Sabbath of Sabbaths". According to Jewish tradition, God inscribes each person's fate for the coming year into a book, the Book of Life, on Rosh Hashanah, and waits until Yom Kippur to "seal" the verdict. During the Days of Awe, a Jewish person tries to amend his or her behavior and seek forgiveness for wrongs done against God [*bein adam leMakom*] and against other human beings [*bein adam lechavero*]. The evening and day of Yom Kippur are set aside for public and private petitions and confessions of guilt [*Vidui*]. At the end of Yom Kippur, one hopes that they have been forgiven by God.

Wikipedia

In the book of Leviticus [Old Testament] we see that the Day of Atonement was a ritualistic practice for the cleansing and washing away of the sins of the people that called for a blood sacrifice being offered up to God by High Priests. These priests, who were themselves imperfect men, had to first offer a sacrifice to atone for their own sin and that of their household before they could even think about going before God on behalf of the people. These ceremonial sacrifices called for the blood of animals [goats, rams, bulls] to be shed; and not just any animal. The sacrifices were required to be pure and unblemished; they had to be the best of the best.

The Ark of the Covenant was housed in the Holy Place behind a veil and only the High Priest were allowed to enter to offer sacrifices, but they couldn't come before the mercy seat of God in just any fashion. They were given explicit instructions as to how they were to prepare to come before the Holy of Holies and if these mandates were not followed to the letter they would die. Once an acceptable sacrifice was prepared the High Priest entered and sprinkled the blood sacrifice on the mercy seat symbolically placing the blood between God and the tablets of the law [The Ten Commandments] which were under the mercy seat. These were the laws which had been broken or transgressed throughout the year. This solemn observance covered the sins of the nation and atonement or forgiveness was granted by God because of it. However, this was only a temporary bandage, if you will, for a continuing situation because this sort of atonement had to be done every year. Can you imagine carrying around a burden for such a time and only being able to "eradicate" it once a year and only through the sacramental sacrifice of someone else's hand?

The sacrifices on the Day of Atonement provided a "covering over" of sin, not a taking away of sin. Christ's blood shed on the cross, however, is God's ultimate atonement for mankind and takes away sin permanently.

Because God desired to save Israel, forgive their sins, and reconcile them to Himself, He furnished a way of salvation by accepting in their place the death of an innocent life [i.e. the animal that was sacrificed.] This animal bore the guilt and penalty and covered their sins by its shed blood, but this was not the end of the story. As Christians we believe that The Day of Atonement is replete with symbolism that foreshadowed the sacrifice of our Lord and Savior Jesus Christ. After a time covering sin with animal sacrifice was no longer acceptable. Jesus Christ came as the Lamb of God to cleanse us from sin, once and for all. He gave of His own life, and shed His own blood, so that rituals and ceremonies were no longer necessary. Jesus gave of Himself so that we would be able to come before the mercy seat ourselves and ask for forgiveness and obtain salvation.

For He made Him who knew no sin to be sin for us, that we might become the righteousness of God in Him.

2 Corinthians 5: 21 [NKJV]

Jesus knows our maladies and frailties and sin nature because He was us. He walked among us. He smelled like us. He was tempted by what we're tempted by. He was hurt by what we're hurt by. He ransomed His own life so that we could be saved. God loved us so much that He gave...and He is still giving, and He's still waiting.

The Old Testament paints a very different picture of the way many of us come to church today. While it has been said with fervor and generosity of intent to "come as you are" this invitation has been taken for granted or even taken out of context in many instances, but thank God for the work of grace in our lives and a better sacrifice, a more permanent sacrifice, and a better covenant or many of us might find death. We come to church out of habit. Once we get there many of us become spectators and not participators. We sit with our mouths closed, arms folded, and legs crossed as if we're expecting to be entertained. We move more and make more noise mimicking Beyoncé or cheering for our favorite sports teams than we do when it comes time to give God the praise He deserves. Many feel that just being "in church" is enough, but I'm here to tell you – it's not. Although God does not require us to present Him with the blood of an animal sacrifice, He does require something. Guess what it is?

I beseech you therefore, brethren, by the mercies of God, that you present your bodies a living sacrifice, holy, acceptable to God, which is your reasonable service. And do not be conformed to this world, but be transformed by the renewing of your mind, that you may prove what is that good and acceptable and perfect will of God.

Romans 12: 1-2 [NKJV]

Guess what else He wants?

Enter into his gates with thanksgiving, and into his
courts with praise: be thankful unto him, and bless his name.

Psalms 100: 4 [NKJV]

Oh, yes. There is something more.

Go out into the highways and hedges, and compel
them to come in, that my house may be filled.

Luke 14:23 [NKJV]

How can we be content to "serve" God when there is
so much chaos erupting around us? Many churches today still
cling to rituals and ceremonies and programs that don't bring
us or anyone else for that matter, any closer to God or
salvation than to the man on the moon.

But Christ came as High Priest of the good things to
come, with the greater and more perfect tabernacle not made
with hands, that is, not of this creation. Not with the blood of
goats and calves, but with His own blood He entered the Most
Holy Place once for all, having obtained eternal redemption.
For if the blood of bulls and goats and the ashes of a heifer,
sprinkling the unclean, sanctifies for the purifying of the flesh,

72

how much more shall the blood of Christ, who through the eternal Spirit offered Himself without spot to God, cleanse your conscience from dead works to serve the living God? And for this reason He is the Mediator of the new covenant, by means of death, for the redemption of the transgressions under the first covenant, that those who are called may receive the promise of the eternal inheritance.

Hebrews 9: 11-15 [NKJV]

Sin, if not atoned for is subject to the wrath and judgment of God.

For the wages of sin is death, but the gift of God is eternal life in Christ Jesus our Lord.

Romans 6:23

The sacrifices on the Day of Atonement provided a "covering up" of sin, not a taking away of sin.

If you have a toothache and the tooth is removed the ache is gone. An ache that is only treated or medicated alleviates the pain momentarily, but the abscessed tooth is still there; much like sin that is only "covered up". Christ paid the full penalty for all sin and effected the conciliation that turns away the wrath of God, reconciles us with Him, and renews our fellowship with Him as the Supreme Sacrifice. Still, even after the horror of the crucifixion, the work had not been fulfilled until the ransomed one ascended to Heaven and presented Himself before a Holy God as the Lamb slain.

Christ was offered once to bear the sins of many. To those who eagerly wait for Him He will appear a second time, apart from sin, for salvation.

Hebrews 9:28 [NKJV]

8

Motive and Spirit

For the Shepherds have become dull-hearted, and have not sought the LORD; therefore they shall not prosper, and all their flocks shall be scattered.

Jeremiah 10:21 [NKJV]

Everything that the Shepherd does must be to the betterment of the sheep. The spirit of the Shepherd speaks to his motives. The sheep are motivated by the Shepherd. If they are guided by a good Shepherd then the spirit of the sheep will be peaceful, fulfilled, and well-tended. This is a collaboration of spirits. If the Shepherd's spirit is contrary to the sheep then the sheep will be unruly. If the sheep know that the Shepherd has their best interests at heart and truly cares for them then they are as one and walk in agreement toward a common goal and purpose. The objective should be to draw the lost to Jesus Christ.

It's past time for us to get real in regard to this Christian walk. It's time out for being seen – we should strive to be relevant. We can go to church every Sunday and run Holy Ghost relays around the walls because the preacher is "sho' nuff preaching", but until we are able to translate that fervor into living in the real world, until Pastors become more concerned about 'Pastoring' the flock and not just auditioning for a spotlight on TBN, then the church as a whole will remain stagnant, teetering toward idol worship while being pacified by a polluted, non-redemptive word. God's intention is for us to live authentic, free, and relatable lives. Admitting our faults and owning up to our failures, but not wallowing in them. We should be able rise above what is around us, but not lose sight of the 'highway, byway dwellers' because, there but for the grace of God go we. *We are in the world, but not of the world.* Having a genuine and transparent relationship with God and man shows those around us that the Holy Ghost is not spooky. We don't float when we walk or speak in tongues 24 hours a day. Being filled with the Spirit of God sometimes is boisterous and demonstrative, but in its most simplistic state it is the verbal expression of our belief that God is God, and that Jesus came and died so that we might gain eternal life through salvation in Christ. That is the basis of Christianity, but it's not a cake-walk. The Holy Ghost sustains us just as air helps us to sustain life as we know it.

These things I have spoken to you, that in Me you may have peace. In the world you will have tribulation; but be of good cheer, I have overcome the world."

John 16:33 [NKJV]

We will face challenges. We will have disappointments, but unlike those who do not know the Lord as Savior we don't have to seek solace in the bottom of a bottle, or at the end of a needle, or in the throes of passion with strangers who could care less about our well-being. Many of us may have been delivered out of similar situations, and should we ever forget, this is where our relationship becomes suspect. Remember our rambunctious brother Peter in Luke the 22nd chapter. Just about the time Jesus was to be offered up as a sacrifice He tells him; *"Simon, Simon! Indeed, Satan has asked for you, that he may sift you as wheat. But I have prayed for you; that your faith should not fail; and when you have returned to Me, strengthen your brethren."*

The prophecy was being fulfilled and Jesus knew full well that Peter would deny ever having known Him, but in love Jesus tells him; *"I have prayed for you that your faith may not fail."*

Let's not forget what God has done in our lives. Let's not forget the dark pit of sin He brought us through so that we would never look down on a brother or sister in need without remembering that we have a similar testimony. That's how we overcome; by the blood of the Lamb and the word of our testimony, not by judgment and self-righteousness.

Likewise the Spirit also helps in our weaknesses. For we do not know what we should pray for as we ought, but the Spirit Himself makes intercession for us with groaning's which cannot be uttered. Now He who searches the hearts knows what the mind of the Spirit is, because He makes intercession for the saints according to the will of God.

And we know that all things work together for good to those who love God, to those who are the called according to His purpose.

Romans 8:26-28 [NKJV]

We should not become so myopic in our walk that we waver when we feel that the servant of God has let us down. We are all imperfect people. God never called anyone who felt they were prepared to do the job, but He has always equipped those whom He called. In truth the amalgamation of the men and women that comprise the church is a flawed fellowship at its worst, but continually pressing toward the mark of the higher calling of Jesus Christ at its best.

God called David when he was just a Shepherd tending the sheep, undoubtedly stinking and dirty just as they were. But, as David grew and became more confident in his calling he was anointed king. An impetuous king. A murderer. A liar. An adulterer. A thief. Even his children committed incest, rape, and attempted murder, but yet in all of that God called David a man after His own heart. Why? Because no matter what David did he knew how to find his way back to God and to the mercy seat of forgiveness. He didn't continue to operate in arrogance believing that he could do no wrong – no harm – he asked God to purge him and clean him up and restore him.

But we are all like an unclean thing, and all our righteousness are like filthy rags; we all fade as a leaf, and our iniquities, like the wind, have taken us away.

Isaiah 64:6 [NKJV]

Man looks on the outside, but God looks on the heart. How many times have you heard that in your lifetime? The heart of man is what God is after. Your inner most being. Your motives. We need to have a heart for what Jesus has a heart for. Only God can take something that is dirty and stinking and sinful and clean it up and transform it into a vessel of honor. We have a responsibility to reveal the truth of Jesus Christ without all the hype and pomposity to those who are spiritually blind and cannot see.

Create in me a clean heart, O God, and renew a steadfast spirit within me. Do not cast me away from Your presence, and do not take Your Holy Spirit from me. Restore to me the joy of Your salvation, and uphold me by Your generous Spirit. Then I will teach transgressors Your ways, and sinners shall be converted to You. Deliver me from the guilt of bloodshed, O God, the God of my salvation, and my tongue shall sing aloud of Your righteousness. O Lord, open my lips, and my mouth shall show forth Your praise. For You do not desire sacrifice, or else I would give it; You do not delight in burnt offering. The sacrifices of God are a broken spirit, a broken and a contrite heart—these, O God, You will not despise.

Psalm 51: 10-17 [NKJV]

The blood of lambs, goats, and bulls are no longer what is required to honor God. The atoning blood of Jesus Christ satisfied that debt on Calvary, but what He does expect – still today – is that the Shepherd as well as the Sheep presents their lives sacrificially to honor Him and bring Him glory. I submit that concept has been lost in the years of prosperity, and name it and claim it, and blab it and grab it. The church as a whole has become a self-centered entity. Online church has become the norm in lieu of a sacred assembly, but God still requires sacrifice.

The giving of ourselves, our time and our resources has been supplanted by the weekly fashion show. In many cases our worship has been contaminated – our sacrifices have been blemished. God still requires pure worship. Our hearts as well as our lives must be presented in sacrifice of this service. We show the world that we are two-faced in our walk when we say one thing and do another. The sheep are chaotic and without order and the Shepherds just want to keep the lights on. Is this true of the entire body of Christ? No. But it is certainly the broad consensus of many who would use the behavior of the saints to avoid the assembly altogether. People en masse are saying that they don't want salvation if it looks like what we're showing them. Our motives are questionable.

Michael W. Smith wrote a song and its melodic chorus simply says; I'm coming back to the heart of worship and it's all about You, It's all about You, Jesus. I'm sorry, Lord, for the thing I've made it when it's all about You; It's all about You, Jesus

We are living in a time, the end time, the last dispensation called Grace, where we need to know beyond the shadow of a doubt that what we stand for and what we do as Christians needs to be all about Jesus Christ, and no one else.

9

GPS

[God's Plan of Salvation]

Guide me, O thou great Jehovah.

Pilgrim through this barren land.

I am weak, but thou are mighty;

Hold me with Thy powerful hand.

Bread of Heaven. Bread of Heaven.

Feed me till I want no more.

Written by William Williams (1717-1791)

Composed by John Hughes (1873-1932)

This is a song I remembered my grandmother singing when I was growing up. In an era when the education of African Americans was forbidden it was songs like this and the comfort of the Word of God that got our forbearers through. Many of our ancestors didn't have much, but they knew how to touch the heart of God. They took comfort in the fact that no matter how hard the journey, or how unforgiving the struggle there was a brighter day ahead. We as a people have lost sight of the fact that this world is not our home. We're devouring all we can here on earth and not looking heaven-ward for much anymore. But, there will come a day of reckoning where we must give an account of the lives that we lead and the souls that we've affected or infected along the way; the sheep that we have led astray or slaughtered with our words or with our deeds.

Ultimately, we are to trust God for guidance and direction, but the model of that trust many times begins with the man or woman who has been assigned to shepherd us. Without God's guidance we are doomed to live a life of confusion and frustration. We'll find ourselves walking in circles and repeatedly going in the wrong direction. Remember the children of Israel and their forty year odyssey in the dessert that could have ended much sooner had they simply followed the directive of God. They clamored and cried for freedom from oppression only to complain about the end result of the methods used to secure that liberty. They loved and followed Moses as long as things were perceived to be well and they were going in the right direction, but many turned on him when the journey to what was promised became difficult. In this case they were given leaders that many bucked against and chose not to follow. They wanted to go their own way and to do their own thing. Sheep that no longer wanted to heed the Shepherd. They created brazen idols to worship, ultimately losing their way. They were returned time and again into captivity until they repented and turned to the God of their salvation and deliverance.

The GPS [Global Positioning Satellite] of today's time is very intuitive for the most part. You program an endpoint and the GPS will tell you turn-by-turn how to get there. When you get off course the device course-corrects until you are back on track. You're alerted when there are roadblocks and traffic congestion and all of this, delays and all, eventually get you to your final destination. How much more intuitive is God's direction for our lives? We get off course. We seek our own agendas. We fall and become captive to sin. We get back up. He brings us out and continues to alert us to roadblocks and pitfalls and this is all designed for His purpose – to bring God glory – and to get us to the place where we are supposed to be.

If any of you lacks wisdom, let him ask of God, who gives to all liberally and without reproach, and it will be given to him. But let him ask in faith, with no doubting, for he who doubts is like a wave of the sea driven and tossed by the wind. For let not that man suppose that he will receive anything from the Lord; he is a double-minded man, unstable in all his ways.

James 1:5-8

God says; "I got this!"

Similar to the relationship between the Shepherd and the sheep, if we stay close to the source of our protection we are the better for it. When we are close to God we not only get spiritual wisdom, God will make us wise to the ways of the world – we'll have discernment. When we are filled with the Spirit of God we can sleep peacefully when everything around us is falling apart. When we feel like we're traversing the wrong path. When life takes us places we thought we'd never be... God says; "I got this!"

"For My thoughts are not your thoughts, nor are your ways My ways," says the LORD. "For as the heavens are higher than the earth, so are My ways higher than your ways, and My thoughts than your thoughts."

Isaiah 55:8 [NKJV]

Remember when Paul and the others were shipwrecked on the island of Malta in Acts 28? I'm sure that was a place that he never thought he'd be, but it was all a part of God's plan. As the story goes Paul was collecting sticks for the fire and a viper latched onto his hand; what was Paul's reaction? He shook it off into the fire and it was consumed. In the course of our journey we will encounter many vipers, or wolves disguised in pretty dresses, three-piece suits, choir robes, or preaching in the pulpit. There have been people we thought were one thing and they ended up being something else. They are the people that try to interfere with our lives and mess up our spirit and ministry. They steer us away from our destiny and purpose, and can become so prominent in our lives that they obscure our view of God. But just like Paul, when they latch onto us we have got to shake them off and get back to purpose.

When we're off course the GPS beeps and an automated voice tells us to make a U-turn when possible; that's one of the functions of the Holy Ghost in our lives. When we wander off we feel a tug in our spirit and a still soft voice urges us to make a U-turn, repent, course correct, go back the right way. If we listen God will keep us from destruction, but if we miss His voice He is still able to keep us and lead and guide us just as the Good Shepherd should. And just when you feel you can't take another step, and life has beaten you and the vipers have sapped all the strength you feel you have. Having done all to stand keep standing because God says; "I got this!"

We must learn to recognize God. We look to see His hand in our circumstances rather than seeking His face. For the most part we are all aware of His conspicuous presence when we come together in church, or in prayer. It's harder to see Him when we're in the dark, or lonely, or going through problems and hardships, but we must trust His plan. We text and tweet, and put our business on Facebook asking strangers, who happen to be on our "friends" list, to pray for the outcome of a particular situation. We seek the council of any and everybody else and call on mama 'nem, making God the last resort. God wants us to trust Him enough to put Him first. How do we recognize God? Instead of worrying or crying and fretting about a thing we need to ask God what it is that He's trying to show us. What is it that He's trying to work out of us or into us, so that we may lay claim to what is His good, acceptable, and perfect will for our lives. A lot of times we want to bind and rebuke the devil for the tribulations, but do you realize you're giving him way too much credit. Satan can only go as far as God allows. The storms come to teach us how to trust God. Trials will come. Hurricane force winds will sometimes blow. Jesus wasn't immune to this and neither will we be if we are to be named His bride. When we cry out to God we may sometimes feel abandoned just as Jesus did when He [who was blameless] was being crucified, but remember this quote from an unknown author; *When you're going through hard times and you wondering where God is, just remember; the teacher is always quiet during a test.* But, if you persevere there is a blessing on the other side of through.

The LORD will guide you continually, and satisfy your soul in drought, and strengthen your bones. You shall be like a watered garden, and like a spring of water, whose waters do not fail.

Isaiah 58:11 [NKJV]

Typically men have a harder time when it comes to following or asking for directions. A lot of marital arguments are born out of pig-headedness. Before GPS came along we'd rather drive around for hours looking for a location when the simple act of humility in asking for help would have solved a lot of problems. As it relates to household projects and furniture or electronic assembly most of us use the picture on the box as a guide and end up with extra pieces that weren't attached and we have no idea where they belong. Consequently when the things we've spent hours on, or sometimes days, don't work or operate in the capacity that it was created for we become discouraged and lose heart. We've all learned the hard way to read and follow directions.

Christians take note. We have a manual; dust it off and open it up if you need to. We don't have to go it alone and end up with extra pieces that don't fit anywhere. If we follow the directions we can be shored up to sustain the weight of the pressures of life and not just flock to what we think is a greener pasture just to have our ears scratched with mere words that aren't walked out with integrity. If we allow the GPS to do what it was designed to do we can and will stay on course, or at the very least not spend forty years trying to figure it out.

Your word is a lamp to my feet and a light to my path.

Psalm 120:105 [NKJV]

10

Covenant Keeper

For if the blood of bulls and goats and the ashes of a heifer, sprinkling the unclean, sanctifies for the purifying of the flesh, how much more shall the blood of Christ, who through the eternal Spirit offered Himself without spot to God, cleanse your conscience from dead works to serve the living God?

Hebrews 9:13, 14 [NKJV]

What is a covenant? I'm glad you asked. A covenant is an agreement between two people to do, or not do something specified. In this case the covenant was between God and man. The covenant of redemption and of restoration.

Were you aware that sheep are mentioned in the Bible over 500 times, more than any other animal? The significance of this grows out of two realities. Sheep were important to the agricultural life of the Hebrews and similar peoples. Secondly, sheep are used throughout the Bible to symbolically refer to God's people. Since the fall of man in the Garden of Eden when curiosity and disobedience out ruled sense and reason it has been God's objective to bring us back into oneness with Him. How is this accomplished? Through a blood sacrifice. As the Lamb of God, Jesus offered Himself up as an atoning sacrifice for our sin and disobedience. God loves us so much that He wrapped Himself in flesh, came down to earth, and took on the sins of all of us so that through the suffering of the cross everlasting redemption could be attained.

But God demonstrates His own love toward us, in that while we were still sinners, Christ died for us.

Romans 5:8 [NKJV]

This is a pretty basic treatise activated by God, but this covenant has been broken many times over, and in this hour we are witness to such things as so called global warming, mass shootings, earthquakes, tsunamis, record snow fall, floods, tornados, and the earth opening up and swallowing people alive. These are all the direct result of our turning away from God in our schools, in our lives and sadly in some of our churches. He wants us to seek His face today just as

He'd told the Israelites of old. You do know why the Israelites stayed in trouble and continued to find themselves in captivity, don't you? Because they didn't heed the words of the Shepherd. They, like most of us, when times are good, want to do our own thing and go our own way. But when the pasture dries up and things get rough and we find ourselves captive and in the midst of crisis and calamity, then we want God's hand in the situation.

But when you hear of wars and rumors of wars, do not be troubled; for such things must happen, but the end is not yet. For nation will rise against nation, and kingdom against kingdom. And there will be earthquakes in various places, and there will be famines and troubles. These are the beginnings of sorrows.

Mark 13: 7, 8 [NKJV]

The catastrophe of the World Trade Center being brought down in New York City, the massacres in Columbine High School, Sandy Hook Elementary, and Lone Star College, shootings in theaters, in churches, and one bomb threat after the other; all of these horrors brought Christians and non-Christians to their knees. Patriotism surges. *In God*

We Trust became more than a pithy little slogan on currency. As unspeakable as these events were they caused a great many of us to call on God like never before. We were praying in the hallowed halls of Washington D.C., and prayer in schools was no longer frowned upon – at least not until the wounds of our national heartache healed and our lives fell back into a pattern of "normalcy".

If My people who are called by My name will humble themselves, and pray and seek My face, and turn from their wicked ways, then I will hear from heaven, and will forgive their sin and heal their land.

2 Chronicles 7:14 [NKJV]

How is it that some of us find it easier to pray when we're in pain? Many of us have made an altar of prayer just about anywhere at any time. We pray in our cars, on the bus, at our desks in school or at work, we find a hallway, we steal away to the restroom, we will find a place to pray in times of distress. I am by no means minimizing the seriousness of our suffering humanity. Could it be that our lack of belief is not at issue, but in times of tremendous loss we want so desperately to believe that we no longer care about being politically correct. We yield to our leaders for guidance. We look to be shepherded. And most of all we just want God to be God.

God wants us to renew the contract we had with Him, Church. We have to humble ourselves and pray and seek His face wholeheartedly and not only His hand, and then we can hear from heaven.

Along with the proliferation of all the mass shootings the subject of gun control in the United States has been front and center. Everyone feels they have the right, as stated in the Constitution, to take up arms. While this is true what's going to happen when lawlessness becomes the rule and we revert to a time resembling the wild, wild, west? Guns don't kill people – people kill people. Taking on this false sense of security is not the whole of the answer. God is waiting on us as a nation, who once proudly stood on the principals of *In God We Trust*, to return to Him. If we want God to heal our land then as the people of God there is something that He requires us to do – pray and then turn from our evil, self-centered – *having* church ways and return to the heart of the only Shepherd that can keep us from falling.

Remember what happened to Sodom when not even ten righteous could be named among them?

Destruction comes; they will seek peace, but there shall be none.

Ezekiel 7:25 [NKJV]

If I might be so bold as to borrow another colloquialism in order to make this a more contemporary argument to ponder; Check yourself before you wreck yourself.

11

A Desperate Cry

Who can be saved? The answer is anyone. Those who are "churched" have most likely heard the phrase from the uttermost to the gutter most. No matter how far you've fallen Jesus still saves.

For the time will come when they will not endure sound doctrine, but according to their own desires, because they have itching ears, they will heap up for themselves teachers; and they will turn their ears away from the truth, and be turned aside to fables.

2 Timothy 4: 3 [NKJV]

Yes, times have changed. Right is wrong. Up is down. Black and white is gray, but Jesus still saves! Isn't that good to know? The only thing that hasn't changed is the requirement for salvation – belief.

If you confess with your mouth the Lord Jesus and believe in your heart that God has raised Him from the dead, you will be saved. For with the heart one believes unto righteousness, and with the mouth confession is made unto salvation.

Romans 10: 9-10 [NKJV]

Like a failing marriage when a husband and wife find communication difficult we just need to remember the passion we once had for Jesus and the comfort we once found in His embrace. Many have found it difficult to believe in the institution of the church whether Catholic, Jewish, Protestant, Pentecostal, or Baptist, but it's not the institution that will save you. It's not the bricks and mortar that will give you comfort. None of us will live forever. At the end of it all there will be certain death. As sure as that reality is, are you just as definite of what is on the other side of it?

Let every man examine himself. Now, even though this particular passage references the taking of communion in memory of the death of Jesus on the cross it should be upheld in every instance. We can blame the Shepherd for his shortcomings. We can blame the sheep for their disinterest, but at the end of it all there is only one image looking back at you when you look in the mirror.

Sometimes it's hard to see things clearly. There is blindness so to speak, but just like Bartimaeus [in the Gospel of Mark], who sat on the side of the Jericho road, once he **heard** that the Shepherd was passing by, began to cry out "Jesus, Son of David, have mercy on me!" He ignored those around him who warned him to be quiet and became more desperate and cried out even louder, "Son of David, have mercy on me!" He didn't care what he looked like. He didn't care how he sounded. He didn't care what the crowd thought of him. He'd been waiting for something and that Great Something had finally come his way. He got the attention he wanted from the only one who mattered. And just like so many countless others, when his faith met the Destiny maker, he received his deliverance.

Do you need help today? Are you feeling hopeless and disjointed? Do you feel like nobody understands you and nobody cares what you're dealing with or going through? Did the Shepherd let you down? Did another sheep disappoint you? In your heart of hearts – when the blame game is over – you know the answer. It's not Prozac, or Jack Daniels, or meth, or cocaine…those are just band aids for the pain. Why not call out for the only true pain reliever? It is not about church membership – it is about faith.

But without faith it is impossible to please Him, for he who comes to God must believe that He is, and that He is a rewarder of those who diligently seek Him.

Hebrews 11:6 [NKJV]

If you've reached the end of your rope tie a knot and hold on. You've come too far to quit. There's nothing of note waiting if you turn around. The Good Shepherd is standing with His arms wide open reminding you to hold on to His unchanging hand. He hears you. He's yet able. He's waiting. Let Him heal you.

12

The Blessings of the Cross

But God forbid that I should boast except in the cross of our Lord Jesus Christ, by whom the world has been crucified to me, and I to the world.

Galatians 6:14 [NKJV]

The source of every God given blessing is found at the cross:

What do you boast in? Let your words stand in judgment of your own life. Whatever you praise is your god. Do you exalt sports teams, athletes, rock stars, rap stars, movies stars, or do you exalt the cross?

"You shall have no other gods before Me."

Exodus 20:3 [NKJV]

Whether it's a person, a possession, a career, bank account or preoccupation with pleasure, if it's between you and Jehovah God it is your small 'g' god. You are being duped by the world, the flesh, the media, and the devil if you find praise in anything else other than the cross. You may say that you believe in God, but until you've experienced the cross of Christ whatever you believe in is a fabricated god. If the cross is not eternal in your life the teachings of Christ may be in your head, but they aren't in your heart. To receive the blessings of the cross Jesus must be in your heart. He must be the center of your joy. And you must boast in the cross of Jesus.

And He shall stand and feed His flock in the strength of the LORD, in the majesty of the name of the LORD His God; and they shall abide, for now He shall be great to the ends of the earth. And this One shall be peace.

Micah 5: 4, 5 [NKJV]

The blessings of peace are found at the cross:

Where is this peace found? This peace is not found in a pill, or a bottle, in pleasure, in wealth, in fortune, in fame, or in power. It is found with reconciliation with God at the cross. It is a peace that surpasses all understanding. There can be no peace of mind until there is peace with God.

Therefore, having been justified by faith, we have peace with God through our Lord Jesus Christ, through whom also we have access by faith into this grace in which we stand, and rejoice in hope of the glory of God. And not only that, but we also glory in tribulations, knowing that tribulation produces perseverance; and perseverance, character; and character, hope.

Romans 5: 1-4 [NKJV]

Shepherds and Sheep alike, it doesn't matter how many times you come to church, how much Bible you can quote, how much money you give, how you raise your hands, shout for joy if you haven't surrendered at the cross and repented of sin and laid it at the cross then you are an enemy of the Father and there will be no peace. Christianity is the call to life, to action, and to involvement. Our lives should be about taking up our cross daily and following Jesus. We should be about putting our hands to the work of the cross and not looking back. Jesus said *"My peace I give you."* The peace of Jesus is greater than the storm. It's greater than the burden or the risk of anything we will ever face in this life.

And you can have it if you want it through the blessings of the cross.

If I regard iniquity in my heart, the Lord will not hear.

Psalm 66:18 [NKJV]

The blessings of prayer are found at the cross:

Do you know what a privilege it is to pray? For some of us, if we leave our iPhone, or iPad, or Androids at home we will turn around and go back to get it. We've got to stay connected even if it costs us an extra 30 minutes of travel time. The privilege of prayer means you're always connected, you don't have to worry about a monthly bill or a dropped call, this is a privilege that is only obtained at the cross and you've got a direct line to the Lord. You don't have to go through anybody's network. Instead of Facebook you can get face-to-face with God. Because of the cross you have the right to lay before God in times of need, struggle, discouragement and trouble and call out; "Father, I stretch my hand to thee. No other help I know." You won't disconnect from me. You won't allow the network to go down. It was because of the sacrificial blessing of the cross that we have been granted direct access to the throne of God. We can go beyond the veil with our prayers and supplications with anticipation and an expectation that God will hear us.

Seeing then that we have a great High Priest who has passed through the heavens, Jesus the Son of God, let us hold fast our confession. For we do not have a High Priest who cannot sympathize with our weaknesses, but was in all points tempted as we are, yet without sin. Let us therefore come boldly to the throne of grace that we may obtain mercy and find grace to help in time of need.

Hebrew 4: 14-16 [NKJV]

The blessings of acceptance are found at the cross:

I will have mercy on her who had not obtained mercy; then I will say to those who were not My people, 'You are My people!' And they shall say, 'You are my God!'"

Hosea 2:23 [NKJV]

The lack of self-esteem is the most notable emotional problem in the country and throughout the world, second only to depression. People are on a desperate search for self-significance. Jesus knows what it's like to be rejected.

He is despised and rejected by men, a Man of sorrows and acquainted with grief. And we hid, as it were, our faces from Him. He was despised, and we did not esteem Him. Surely He has borne our griefs and carried our sorrows; yet we esteemed Him stricken. Smitten by God, and afflicted, but He was wounded for our transgressions. He was bruised for our iniquities. The chastisement for our peace was upon Him. And by His stripes we are healed. All we like sheep have gone astray. We have turned, every one, to his own way. And the LORD *has laid on Him the iniquity of us all.*

Isaiah 53:3-6 [NKJV]

From the moment He was born until his death on the cross Jesus faced constant rejection from His people. Even in the last moments of His life He looked up into the face of the only One He truly trusted and said; "My God! My God! Why have *You* forsaken Me?" He knows what rejection is all about.

Perhaps you've been rejected by a spouse, or a son or daughter, your parents, or somebody you thought had your back, but there is someone who loves you so much that He sent His only begotten Son all the way to the cross to die so that you can have everlasting life and that you might have a friend that sticks closer than a brother. Jesus promised to never leave or forsake us. His arms are extended today in acceptance. He says; "The one that comes to Me I will by no means cast out." He will wrap His arms around you and you will never feel dejected again. The loving Shepherd. The caring Shepherd. Jesus loves us in spite of our imperfections and downfalls. He loves us because He is love. Jesus accepts you when no one else will. His love is pure, rich, measureless, and eternal. You are accepted at the cross. Love is plentiful at the cross. Blessings overflow at the cross.

At the cross, at the cross where I first saw the light,
And the burden of my heart rolled away,
It was there by faith I received my sight,
And now I am happy all the day!

Isaac Watts, *pub.* 1707
ref. by Ralph E. Hudson, 1885

13

Nothing But The Blood

What then shall we say to these things? If God is for us, who can be against us? He who did not spare His own Son, but delivered Him up for us all, how shall He not with Him also freely give us all things? Who shall bring a charge against God's elect? It is God who justifies. Who is he who condemns? It is Christ who died, and furthermore is also risen, who is even at the right hand of God, who also makes intercession for us. Who shall separate us from the love of Christ? Shall tribulation, or distress, or persecution, or famine, or nakedness, or peril, or sword?

Romans 8: 31-35[NKJV]

I am forgiven because of the blood. I am healed because of the blood. I have peace because of the blood. I have everlasting life because of the blood. I am who I am because of the blood. Christ went to the cross and completed his task, and forever defeated Satan. Every blessing I have is because. There are no blessings, not now or ever, for any other reason except for the redemptive blood of Jesus. As Christians our reality is Christ. We are saved because of Him in whom we believe. We have hope for an eternity in Heaven because we rejoice in His resurrection. The Easter Bunny has never saved anybody. There is no power in the painted eggs or the flavored jelly beans. One day, Shepherds and sheep, goats, wolves and snakes alike will stand before the Almighty God all because of the blood.

For it is written:

"As I live, says the LORD, every knee shall bow to Me, and every tongue shall confess to God." So then each of us shall give account of himself to God.

Romans 14: 11. 12 [NKJV]

We can't boast about stained glass windows, buildings, and programs and budgets, but we can boast in the blood. The blood will never lose its power. You may think you have it going on but you don't have anything unless you've been washed in the blood of the Lamb.

As it is written:

"For Your sake we are killed all day long; we are accounted as sheep for the slaughter." Yet in all these things we are more than conquerors through Him who loved us. For I am persuaded that neither death nor life, nor angels nor principalities nor powers, nor things present nor things to come, nor height nor depth, nor any other created thing, shall be able to separate us from the love of God which is in Christ Jesus our Lord.

Romans 8: 36-39 [NKJV]

Through the blood of Jesus we are overcomers. Yes, you know all of this. You can quote chapter and verse daily, but do you really *know* it? Do you *know* that the same blood that saved you is able to keep you? Is this the message that we are still declaring to the lost sheep? Or has this message given way to simply *having church*?

There is *power* in the blood. What can wash away my sin…nothing but the blood of Jesus. What can make me whole again? I don't care how devout you are sometimes you can feel a little bit broken You can feel like you're doing everything you know how to do and still have the sense of brokenness, but that's when you can come to the Shepherd and cry out to be made whole again, to be restored, to be renewed. There is still *power* in the blood!

Don't believe me? If your blood is drained from your body, then your organs will shut down and you'll die. The blood carries oxygen to every part of your body. Your body has to have blood and if your blood is tainted you have to have a blood transfusion. I've got news for you; we all had contaminated blood, but when you stopped by Calvary and gave your life to Jesus you received a blood transfusion, and a transfer was made in the Spirit. Your sin, your mistakes, your self-loathing, your judgmental attitudes, and all your other maladies were covered by the blood of Jesus Christ. Don't you think that is good news worth sharing?

Here's my testimony; I've only been in the hospital twice in my life; once for a ruptured artery, the second time with a strange viral ulcer. I was hemorrhaging for six months. I was preaching like a wild man, teaching Bible study every Wednesday night – for six months. One night after my shower I passed out. I got up and spit up black blood. My wife came to check on me and I chocked it up to food poisoning. I got back in the shower, cleaned up and then I got into bed. When I got up I was started spitting up again. The hemorrhaging was so substantial that it looked and felt as if I was completely depleted of blood. My wife insisted that I was going to the hospital, but I needed to take another shower. By this time I was going down for the count. In my weakened state I was dressed and offered no resistance as I was being attended to. When we got to the ER the doctor was astounded that I was still alive. I was rushed into surgery and I asked the Elders to pray. The doctor insisted that he needed to operate [but like the woman with the blood flow problems in the eighth chapter of Luke] I needed God to dry this thing up. I was taken to the operating room and put under anesthesia and shortly thereafter they woke me back up. I asked my wife what they did because I didn't feel like anything had been done. I was told that by the time they went down into my throat with some sort of laparoscopic device they found that the ulcer had dried up the size of a raisin. They didn't get a chance to do anything because there was nothing to do. They were dumbfounded by the fact that my body didn't shut down and I didn't suffer brain damage. But I knew that even though there is regenerative power in the natural blood, it is not the same resurrection power that is in the blood of Jesus. Everything moves by the Spirit of God, and there is nothing like the blood of the Lamb.

Hallelujah! Glory to God!

14

Business As Usual Is No Longer Acceptable

And as it was in the days of Noah, so it will be also in the days of the Son of Man: They ate, they drank, they married wives, they were given in marriage, until the day that Noah entered the ark, and the flood came and destroyed them all. Likewise as it was also in the days of Lot: They ate, they drank, they bought, they sold, they planted, they built; but on the day that Lot went out of Sodom it rained fire and brimstone from heaven and destroyed them all. Even so will it be in the day when the Son of Man is revealed.

Luke 17:26-30 [NKJV]

In these terrifying times God is calling the church into a greater accountability. In many cases we've gone so far away from the Bible and the foundation of the Word that we think it is okay to continue on the same path that we're on. As God said in Haggai chapter one, when the people went about building up their own lives, now is the time for us to consider our ways.

In the body of Christ we love the mantras that we feel will ignite the congregation. We will at times get carried away with the catchphrase; God is doing a new thing. But in reality, because we refuse to shift our paradigm the "we've always done it this way" mentality creeps back in and there really isn't much new about it. Sure, the leaders will stand before a particular flock with their own versions of the state of their union and proclaim a new day, and a new direction and in earnest the new gets trotted out for a while, but once this illusion fades we fall back into the same old patterns.

Jesus had essentially one sermon. Everything He did and said revolved around one message. Which was; the kingdom of heaven is at hand. Jesus reminded those who exercised power of any kind on earth that they did not have the last word. He informed them that with His coming and in His person God was about to do something refreshing. God was about to do something radical – something which would be liberating and which would challenge old ways of doing and thinking about things. Jesus came to call the powers that be into question and put them on notice that business as they had been doing it, business as they knew it; business as usual was no longer acceptable.

Every miracle Jesus performed established His supremacy over forces and systems that believed they had the last word regarding the human predicament. Every time Jesus chose to reinterpret a religious tradition He showed that even the law and the prophets found their fulfillment in Him. Jesus came to declare that a new day was dawning. Having church service as usual, going through the motions as usual, doing the same thing week after week would not be tolerated.

But you are a chosen generation, a royal priesthood, a holy nation, His own special people, that you may proclaim the praises of Him who called you out of darkness into His marvelous light;

1 Peter 2:9 [NKJV]

Let's be clear; it is the Christ that is in us that is the hope of glory. The world has to see a difference in the church. They **must** see a difference. No lost sheep can be found if we're not looking. No lost sheep can been cared for if all we care about is ourselves; what we have, what we wear, how we drive, or how we live. Speaking of living, we ought to know that our living absolutely needs to be a reflection of Jesus

118

Christ – that is after all the heart and soul of who we are to be. Subsequently, we need to smell like Jesus.

Hypocrisy is yet another reason people en masse shun the church. Prolific preachers are so eloquent and convincing that they figuratively preach the paint off the walls. Choirs and soloist are singing and running melodic scales until the light fixtures shake. Congregations are running, screaming, shouting, and throwing money at the altar in a ritualistic frenzy. No tangible deliverance is wrought – no lives are changing – those that come don't stay – those that stay don't repent. We have to do more than sing and preach about this Jesus. Business as usual is no longer acceptable.

"What man of you, having a hundred sheep, if he loses one of them, does not leave the ninety-nine in the wilderness, and go after the one which is lost until he finds it? And when he has found it, he lays it on his shoulders, rejoicing. And when he comes home, he calls together his friends and neighbors, saying to them, 'Rejoice with me, for I have found my sheep which was lost!' I say to you that likewise there will be more joy in heaven over one sinner who repents than over ninety-nine just persons who need no repentance. "Or what

woman, having ten silver coins, if she loses one coin, does not light a lamp, sweep the house, and search carefully until she finds it? And when she has found it, she calls her friends and neighbors together, saying, 'Rejoice with me, for I have found the piece which I lost!' Likewise, I say to you, there is joy in the presence of the angels of God over one sinner who repents."

Luke 15: 1-10 [NKJV]

The book of Luke goes on to talk about the prodigal son who left his father's house believing he was grown enough to do what he wanted to do how he wanted to do it [you know how we do]. But when he'd spent all his money and had sunk as low as anybody could sink he got himself together and went home. Did his father shun him? No. He welcomed him back with open arms and prepared the best of what he had to show him how much he'd been missed and that he was still loved.

Those succinct stories illustrate instructive principles, or lessons that mirror the basis of what being Christ-like is all about.

The Bible says *we are the salt of the earth*, but not a block of salt. A block of salt can't savor or season anything. There needs to be some shaking going on and salt can't be shaken if its clumped and compacted together; coagulating and hardened against the bleating, and the cries of the sheep. We need to be fluid and usable or all the singing and the preaching and the gathering together is a huge waste of time and energy. We may as well do like those who'd rather not be bothered; stay home, sleep in, wash the car, walk the dog, do laundry, anything we can find to do that doesn't revolve around a church meeting.

There are some in the church that have a selfish need to keep things as they've always been. The Pharisees, with their vested interest, came to Jesus and asked him about this new kingdom that would come. They were worried about His crusade – that it would change things with regards to their very familiar and habitual style of worship. Those with interests in maintaining the status quo, whether in the church or in the community, are always the ones most concerned about change and how it will affect their itinerary. Undoubtedly because they feel that they personally have the most to lose by change. You can't really be comfortable folding your arms, crossing your legs, and spectating if the Spirit of God wants to do a new thing.

Many sheep are still scattered to the four winds. Not knowing who or what to believe and not trusting anyone. They are searching for answers, looking for truth. What is the response of the church as it exists today? All too often it is simply business as usual. We are busy planning our programs, having concerts and anniversaries while the world is dying and moving closer to drawing its final breath. We're closer than we've ever been before, and we blithely go about our normal routines. It's time out for merely assembling inside of a building and leaving out exclaiming "we had church today." The church is supposed to be represented in all of us. We need to decide now that we are going to be agents of change and the disciples that we have been called to be. We have to transition from talking about it and be about it. We must be like the voice of John the Baptist, crying out in the wilderness against the hostility and indifference many face. We must urge the misplaced flock to come home. We can broker change and hope and help for the hurting and those who are bound by the demonic systems of this age. In a world where tolerance has become the new religion, we have to engage in the fight for the lost.

For the weapons of our warfare are not carnal but mighty in God for pulling down strongholds, casting down arguments and every high thing that exalts itself against the knowledge of God, bringing every thought into captivity to the obedience of Christ.

2 Corinthians 10: 4, 5 [NKJV]

STOP! Let's stop eating and drinking, buying and selling, planting and building just for the sake of doing. Jesus said *in that day*; many are going to say to me, Lord didn't we prophesy in your name? Didn't we cast out demons in your name? Didn't we preach in your name? Didn't we sing to your glory? And the most terrible response he could give us is; "Depart from me. I don't know you! Get out of my face you who work iniquity!" After years and years of "having church", and singing in the choir, and preaching, and giving, is that the kind of response you want to hear from the God who has the power of life and death in His hands.

Sadly, some of us are going to lose our souls and go to hell from some church choir, some church board, some church auxiliary, and yes, some pulpit doing the same thing we've always done and not allowing for the move of God. Albert Einstein said that the very definition of insanity is doing the same thing over and over and expecting different results. How can we expect to win the lost if we continue church as usual? How do we expect to retrieve scattered sheep if we don't go out there where they are?

What are we doing if we're not devoting our lives to being better, helping to build stronger Christians, or shepherding those who would come into join us? What are we doing? The world is going to hell in a basket and the basket is on fire. Business as usual is unacceptable! The church must do more. We must do more than play politics and jockey for position. We must do more than campaign for titles. We must do more than chase after the preacher with what they've deemed to be a *rhema* word, or the choir or gospel artists with the hottest voices. We are called to change the world. We must be a light in darkness. We must be the salt of the earth.

The Sheep

Ultimately I believe there is a need for a place for believers to gather to encourage one another and regroup to face and minister to the world. I think that place should be a refuge; a place of healing, acceptance and love. That is the ideal. How we get there seems to escape us as the body of Christ. I don't want to believe this is so, but my past experience with the "organization" has left me cold. I don't confuse the failure of the institution as a failure of our Father. His word is clear on love being a more excellent way. There has to be a balance between the wonderful edifice and structured organization and going out into the highways and byways to minister to the lost. We can't be so consumed with making the mortgage and salaries over reaching out to the surrounding community and really becoming that city that is set on a hill. The church should be synonymous with kindness, help, safety, shelter and not in-fighting and scandal, and ridicule. We have to stop being the punch line and become the standard bearers for what is right and pure and true. I continue to pray and hope to see that model realized. This is just my simple opinion. Lord I believe. Help my unbelief.

15

The Return of the Ultimate Shepherd

Many of the church of old used to say "this world is not my home." As Christians we are living to live again. The ultimate victory – our goal – our destiny is HEAVEN.

For the Lord Himself will descend from heaven with a shout, with the voice of an archangel, and with the trumpet of God. And the dead in Christ will rise first. Then we who are alive and remain shall be caught up together with them in the clouds to meet the Lord in the air. And thus we shall always be with the Lord. Therefore comfort one another with these words.

1 Thessalonians 4:16-18 [NKJV]

We as a church need revival. I'm not just talking about another special service with a guest preacher that comes and whips us into yet another spiritual frenzy. I'm talking about a real revival, a renewing of our minds, souls, and spirit. We need to have a reawakening of our zeal for the manifest presence of God among us when we come together in worship both corporately and in our personal time with Him.

Psalms tells us that we are His people and the sheep of His pasture. God's sheep. God's pasture. Most wayward sheep that have bounced from church to church and chased after the next *hot* word over the course of a lifetime have spent way too much time grazing in the wrong pastures; looking to a man or woman for something that can only be found in God. We know that it is God that gives us those men and women who are to undergird and under-Shepherd His flock until His impending and glorious return, but so many have been damaged and hurt and assaulted that it has become nearly impossible to know who to believe. Can we trust what our eyes see or what our ears are hearing?

Where does this all leave us? Right back to where we started. Available, Accessible, Approachable, and Accountable. We are all accountable for the things we do in this life. One day we will all stand in judgment for the lives we touched both negatively and positively. At the end of your journey would you rather hear God say "Well done." Or would you rather Him say; depart from me."

As the Bible is being fulfilled before our very eyes the return of the Good Shepherd is imminent. We are living in the last dispensation, the last age, which is the church age. There will be no other. Christ's return must be paramount in our teaching. Unfortunately, too many Shepherds are not preparing their flocks for this impending occurrence. On the whole we are not teaching it, not preaching, not admonishing, not embracing, nor endorsing it. We're spending far too much time on building programs, seed sowing, and media exposure, rather than making ready for the appearing of our Christ – the Good Shepherd. He that has an ear let him hear what the Spirit is saying to the church.

"Surely I am coming quickly." Amen. Even so, come, Lord Jesus!

Revelation 22:20 [NKJV]

Behold, He is coming with clouds, and every eye will see Him, even they who pierced Him. And all the tribes of the earth will mourn because of Him. Even so, Amen.

Revelation 1:7 [NKJV]

Now unto that same sweet Jesus, who was manifested in the flesh, justified in the Spirit, seen of angels and received in glory! May He bless His saints now henceforth and forevermore!

Get right church and let's go home!

"One day Jesus is coming! You may be at church! You may be at work! You may be asleep! God grant that you would be ready when He makes His personal appearance.

What if His appearance occurs…on a Sunday Morning?"

Sunday Morning Rapture

2013 International Christian Film Festival

4th place winner

Available now on Amazon.com or can be ordered through EndTouchMovies.net

ABOUT THE AUTHORS

Dr. William L. Sheals

Dr. William L. Sheals, Spirit-filled teacher, great visionary, loving, and dedicated pastor are all words that adequately describe this great man of God, Bishop William Sheals. "Papa Sheals", as he's known by his flock, because of the fatherly, AGAPE love and compassion that he shows toward each of his members, is the senior pastor, for over 31 years, of Hopewell Missionary Baptist Church in Norcross, GA.

Bishop Sheals, a Lakeland, FL native, came to Hopewell Missionary Baptist Church in May 1980. Under his direction and leadership, Hopewell grew from a small rural church to a suburban mega-church. Bishop Sheals is extremely grateful to God for blessing this great union of pastor and church for over 32 years, which is rarely heard of in today's religious communities. In 1990, God gave Bishop Sheals a great vision of transforming a 32 acre junk yard, into a beautiful complex where God would be glorified. He wrote the vision and printed it for all to see. After much prayer and hard work, this great vision began to manifest in 1992. Today this awesome community is known as the "City of Hope" which houses a Child Development Center, Youth Center, Senior Citizen Center and Adult Fitness Center, and Mall with a beauty & barber salon, caterer, bakery and a print shop. The mall also has an employment service called "Hope for the Future." However, it doesn't stop there. The City of Hope also has a fully accredited beautiful Christian

Academy where children from K4 - 12th grade are educated. The campus also boasts an accredited Bible College.

His entertainment business credits include:
• Broadway/Off-Broadway experience in the 1960's
• Radio station personality and station owner - 1970's
• Three major film appearances
• Director of two Independent films
• "The Prodigal Son - Written, directed and produced.

Bishop Sheals has written over 7 inspirational books and has received numerous awards and honors such as the Presidential Special Citizens Award for "Founding Director of Ministers Against Drugs" in 1989, Founding

president of the N. Metro 100 Black Men in 1993, recipient of the Martin Luther King, Jr. Drum Major Award in 1999, and Who's Who in Black America in 2002, and most recently Bishop Sheals received the Gwinnett County NCCAP Lifetime Achievement Award. He is currently serving as Ambassador of Reconciliation and Goodwill for Israel and is also acknowledged in History Maker's African American History Archive.

Bishop Sheals is fun-loving and conservative with a great sense of humor. He is happily married to Patricia and they have two children Ryan and Ari.

Eric Ayala

Eric Ayala is a multi-faceted and gifted writer, director, author, actor, singer, and producer.

He's been published in 3 genres – all 3 pseudonyms he uses are variations of his full name.

Writing in the genre of Inspirational fiction and using the penname E.L. Ayala his first book Restoration was published in 1997. Then in 1998 he wrote, directed and produced the stage play *Will You Be Made Whole* which debuted on stage at the 14th Street Playhouse. The play was followed later that year with what was to become the first in the wholeness series.

The book Will You Be Made Whole was followed by the success of the sequel Alabaster Box…Two Women One Struggle, and then

…if i should die before i wake. *Will You Be Made Whole* [the play] continued to perform well over the next 3 years. Eric is currently working on the 4th book of the series entitled ...an issue of blood.

* In 2003 his contemporary musical *The Women* debuted and sold out 2 performances at the Morton Theatre in Athens, Georgia.

In 2010 Eric facilitated a writing workshop and met Ms. Cynthia Artis who tasked him to write and direct the phenomenal Black History Month production of *Strange Fruit* for Hopewell Christian Academy. While working on the stage play he was introduced to Dr. William L. Sheals, who was also cast in *Strange Fruit*. Dr. Sheals hired Eric to write the screenplay for *Sunday Morning Rapture*, and brought him on as an Assistant Director. The movie *Sunday Morning Rapture* made its acclaimed premiere at the Fabulous Fox Theatre in Atlanta, GA in November 2011.

Eric's stage and musical credits include The Music Man, Joseph and the Amazing Technicolor Dreamcoat, Dreamgirls, Porgy and Bess, Pacific Overtures, Lucia Di Lammermoor, Don Giovanni, and Il Trovatore.

In addition to all of that he still finds the time to work with other authors and playwrights on various projects and freelance for Good Catch Publishing.

His dedicates his craft and love for words to his mother Elizabeth.

"I know without God I could do nothing, and I most definitely would be nothing."

Made in the USA
Charleston, SC
05 February 2014